Exploring Music as Worship and Theology

D1280338

AMERICAN ESSAYS IN LITURGY

SERIES EDITOR, EDWARD FOLEY

Exploring Music as Worship and Theology

Research in Liturgical Practice

Mary E. McGann, R.S.C.J.

THE LITURGICAL PRESS
Collegeville, Minnesota

www.litpress.org

1	2	3	4	5	6	7	8	9

Library of Congress Cataloging-in-Publication Data

McGann, Mary E.
    Exploring music as worship and theology : research in liturgical practice / Mary E. McGann.
        p.   cm. — (American essays in liturgy)
    Includes bibliographical references.
    ISBN 0-8146-2824-9 (alk. paper)
    1. Church music—Catholic Church—Cross-cultural studies.
2. Catholic Church—Liturgy—Research—Methodology.   I. Title.
II. American essays in liturgy (Collegeville, Minn.)

ML3080.M34   2002
264'.2—dc21   2001038825

Contents

Introduction

This volume is about *method*—a method for exploring music as worship and theology within the lived faith experience of worshiping communities. As such, it is a book about *persons*—persons and communities who make music in culturally distinct ways, and through their music express their existence before God. It is about *scholars*, who look to the liturgical performance of local assemblies to discover how the churches' living traditions of worship and faith are being received, shaped, and handed on at this moment in history. This book is about *musicians* committed to a deeper understanding of the diverse cultural musics erupting within our churches—musical systems that need to be comprehended on their own terms and that cannot be adequately understood through the forms or categories of the Western musical system. It is about *cultural borderlands* and *border crossings*—the borderlands between the diverse ethno-cultural and religious traditions that coalesce within our ecclesial bodies; the borderlands between the worlds of academia and the sphere of human living; the intersection between theory-making, music-making, and ritual-making; the borderlands between the several academic disciplines necessary for the study of liturgical-musical performance; and the border crossings that must take place for these worlds to inform each other. Finally, this book is about *doing liturgical theology*—about who will be engaged in our conversations about the meanings of liturgical-musical performance and how new members of the field might be prepared for their future tasks.

Methods without persons make little sense. Methods for studying musical and liturgical performance are deceptive if they keep us from the rich human encounter they are meant to support. The method presented in this essay was born within the dynamic encounter between the author and a predominantly African American

Catholic community—a community which, for the past three decades, has shaped a ritual-musical confluence of its complex identity as both Black and Roman Catholic. The method was honed in studies of liturgical theology, ethnomusicology, and ritual studies—used and revised in four years of field research. It is offered here to encourage others to pursue similar modes of research. What matters ultimately is neither our methods nor our research, but the breadth of understanding, respect, and informed appreciation they yield.

In the early 1990s, I first met the community of Our Lady of Lourdes in San Francisco. The performance of Black gospel music is central to the worship of this predominantly African American community. Within their liturgy, gospel performance is a carrier of profound intuitions about God's action in the Spirit and of ritual assumptions about how the community engages in liturgy. It is a rich communication of their ethno-cultural and religious history and identity. Historically, gospel music developed within the worship performance of the African American Church, quite independently of Catholic settings. It flourished in the often hostile urban environments of the northern United States to which African Americans migrated in the 1920s and 1940s. Powerfully religious in its intent, gospel music harnesses rhythms and stylistic elements shared with a range of secular musics to speak a message of faith in the most concrete of human situatedness. In four years of field research, done with the blessing of the Our Lady of Lourdes community and its musical and pastoral leaders, I sought to discover the full impact of this vital musical style on their Catholic liturgy and on the embodied theology that emerges in their musical performance.[1] Given my own formation as a Roman Catholic woman of Irish American descent, and my professional training in both liturgy and music, this experience was for me a rich and challenging learning process.

Gospel music is only one of the many cultural musics finding a home in the liturgical assemblies of our various denominations. Massive cultural changes and processes of globalization impact our Christian communities here and in other parts of the world. As we stretch to embrace a global church, these cultural musics take their

---

[1] All references to the Our Lady of Lourdes community in this volume, including illustrations from their worship, are used with permission. See Mary McGann, "Interpreting the Ritual Role of Music in Christian Liturgical Practice" (Ph.D. diss., Graduate Theological Union, 1996) 71–244.

place alongside the idioms of the Western musical system that has shaped many traditions of Christian worship. They are important indicators of religious growth and liturgical change: a Latino community singing *cantos*, accompanied by a *conjunto* or *Mariachi* ensemble; an Indian assembly singing *bhajan* to the accompaniment of *tablā* and harmonium; a Vietnamese assembly chanting sacred texts and prayers in *đọc kinh*—an a capella form of chanting based on the tonal scale of the Vietnamese language.[2] Each idiom is not only an acoustic/sonic tradition, but a carrier of social customs, of ritual expectations, of spirituality, and of cosmology. But how can we access these musics as complex systems of meaning and explore the manner in which they are used by Christian assemblies? How can we understand these emerging dimensions of our liturgical heritage?

The study of liturgical performance has been part of liturgical scholarship for several decades. In the 1970s, Mary Collins invited scholars to study the particularity of communities' faith expression in worship.[3] She drew on the work of several ritual theorists to expand the frameworks liturgical scholars use to interpret Christian worship, calling attention to the non-verbal dimensions as critical to the meanings set out in our liturgical rites. Collins posited that ritual assemblies, which "have been and continue to be the point of sustained contact with mystery," are a prime, if neglected, theological source. In 1983, Mark Searle invited the North American Academy of Liturgy to pursue actively a new branch of liturgical studies, namely "pastoral liturgical studies." The purpose of this field would be the collection of empirical and interpretive data about the worship practice of particular communities that could reveal "how the symbolic words and gesture of the liturgy operate when they engage the believing community."[4] A few years later, Searle and others conducted a major sociological study of Catholic parishes in the

---

[2] Examples taken from: Mark P. Bangert, "Liturgical Music, Culturally Tuned," *Liturgy and Music: Lifetime Learning*, ed. Robin A. Leaver and Joyce Ann Zimmerman (Collegeville: The Liturgical Press, 1998) 370–6; Rufino Zaragoza, "A New Millennium: We've Been There Before," *The Way of St. Francis* 5:5 (1999) 32. *Đọc kinh*, also referred to as *bài ca nguyên*, is performed antiphonally between the one who presides and the rest of the assembly.

[3] See her *Worship: Renewal to Practice* (Washington, D.C.: Pastoral Press, 1987) 57–134.

[4] Mark Searle, "New Tasks, New Methods: The Emergence of Pastoral Liturgical Studies," *Worship* 57:4 (1983) 300.

United States, which gave central focus to the worship of communities included.[5] Margaret Mary Kelleher, writing in 1988, underscored the centrality of liturgical praxis for the work of liturgical theology, and offered a method for observing/interpreting the ritual performance of particular assemblies.[6] Kelleher's own study of Catholic liturgical performance, as well as her writing on ritual studies and hermeneutics, continues to provide a grounding for further empirical research.[7] Rebecca Slough expanded the horizon of studies of liturgical performance through research into the performed prayer styles of several Free Church congregations.[8]

These approaches assume that liturgy, by its nature, is performative—that it exists only in performance. They call attention to the theologies of worship that are deeply embedded in the action of particular communities. They represent a broadening of the models and methods used in liturgical studies—from a predominantly normative paradigm to models that include empirical research based on methods drawn from the social and human sciences. They shift the attention of liturgical scholars from a primary focus on the "doctrinal efficacy" of rites to their "operational efficacy" for particular cultural communities.[9] As yet, however, little has been done to develop methods for studying music within a community's worship

---

[5] Mark Searle and David Leege, *Notre Dame Study of Catholic Parish Life* (Notre Dame, Ind.: University of Notre Dame Press, 1985).

[6] Margaret Mary Kelleher, "Liturgical Theology: A Task and a Method," *Worship* 62:1 (1988) 2–25.

[7] See Margaret Mary Kelleher, "The Communion Rite: A Study of Roman Catholic Liturgical Performance," *Journal of Ritual Studies* 5:2 (1991) 99–122; idem., "Liturgy as Source for Sacramental Theology," *Questions liturgiques* 72 (1991) 33–5; idem., "Hermeneutics in the Study of Liturgical Performance," *Worship* 67:4 (1993) 292–31; idem., "Ritual Studies and the Eucharist: Paying Attention to Performance," *Eucharist: Toward the Third Millennium* (Chicago: Liturgy Training Publications, 1997) 51–64.

[8] Rebecca Jo Slough, "A Method for Describing the Practice and Theology of Worship: A Study of Prayer in Three Free Church Congregations" (Ph.D. diss., Graduate Theological Union, 1989).

[9] See Michael B. Aune, "The Return of the Worshiper to Liturgical Theology: Studies of the Doctrinal and Operational Efficacy of the Church's Worship" (unpublished, 1992) 4–8. Aune borrows these terms from Barbara Meyerhoff and Sally Falk Moore, *Secular Ritual* (Amsterdam: Van Gorcum, Assen, 1977) 10–15.

performance, and for assessing how a community's musical perform-ance affects the entire continuum of liturgical action, shaping and expressing an embodied theology.[10]

This essay addresses that challenge. The method I propose as-sumes that music is a constitutive part of a community's liturgical prayer. Its purpose is to enable an exploration of music *as worship* and *as theology* through the focused study of music in the ritual per-formance of particular communities. The method is necessarily interdisciplinary. Each of the three fields of liturgical studies, ethno-musicology, and ritual studies offers us a different yet complemen-tary view of what takes place when a liturgical assembly makes music. Taken together, the perspectives, theories, and methods of these three disciplines provide a basis for studying and interpreting music as an integral part of liturgical performance. They enable us to explore an assembly's worship music as carrier of religious, spir-itual, cultural, and theological meanings, and as central to how a community shapes and hands on its liturgical tradition. It is my hope that other scholars will take up the work of studying worship music, using all or parts of this method, or developing comparable methods of their own. The approach I take can be used in a variety of cultural and denominational settings, and can be adapted to a range of musical idioms.

My focus in this essay is on the fruitfulness of this research for the field of liturgical studies. However, attention to the music of one or more communities might bear fruit in other fields of study as well, namely pastoral theology and ethics. Practically, such research may enlighten parish or diocesan leaders as they negotiate the chal-lenges of liturgical inculturation. For example, studies using this method might provide a basis for sensitive and inclusive planning within multicultural parishes. Or they might ground the work of a music and liturgy commission in a diocese where new cultural mu-sics have been introduced into the worship of member parishes. I invite readers to explore these uses as well.

Chapter 1 lays an interdisciplinary foundation for the research process and interpretive strategies that will be explored in the re-mainder of the book. Orientations from the fields of liturgical studies,

[10] See Edward Foley's comments on the need for field work in liturgical music, "Liturgical Music: A Bibliographic Essay," *Liturgy and Music: Lifetime Learning,* ed. Robin A. Leaver and Joyce Ann Zimmerman (Collegeville: The Liturgical Press, 1998) 450–1.

11

ethnomusicology, and ritual studies are offered as starting points for exploring what takes place when liturgical assemblies make music. I have woven together numerous insights from theorists in each field, yet these in no way exhaust the resources of each discipline for those studying musical-ritual performance. Sources cited in the footnotes may serve as a springboard for further study and reflection.

Based on these orientations, Chapter 2 presents a research process by which scholars/practitioners might access and interpret a community's musical-liturgical performance. It articulates the starting points, the tasks, and the "communities of accountability" that compose the research field. It delineates appropriate tools, procedures, and resources for describing, analyzing, and interpreting a community's practice. It discusses appropriate modes for presenting the research to a wider scholarly or pastoral audience. Finally, it addresses the challenging ethical questions: Who stands to benefit from this research and how? Does the information we seek as scholars truly enrich not only our discipline but the persons who welcome us into their communal worship and music making?

Chapter 3 offers a model for how research into the worship music of particular communities might be integrated into the work of liturgical studies, or by implication, into the pastoral frameworks of another group. The model offered in this last phase of the method is that of a creative dialogue—a dialogue between the academic or pastoral community that receives the research and the researcher(s), who "speaks with" the community studied. Here I explore how the dialogue might take place, who might be engaged in the collaborative reflection, and what might provide a basis for their conversation. I believe this dialogue is crucial as we embark on the new millennium and navigate the increased cultural and liturgical change occurring in our ecclesial bodies. Throughout the chapter, I use selected illustrations from my own field research. These do not exhaust the learnings of the research, but anticipate a fuller presentation of the community's experience in a subsequent volume.[11] Finally, I offer brief reflections on the implications of the method for the field of liturgical studies and for how future liturgical scholars might be prepared for their task.

[11] *A Precious Fountain: Music in the Worship of an African American Catholic Community* (forthcoming).

1 Interdisciplinary Orientations to Musical-Liturgical Practice

This chapter sets an interdisciplinary framework within which to carry out the study of a community's musical-liturgical practice. Each of the three fields of liturgical studies, ethnomusicology, and ritual studies offers resources for accessing and interpreting what takes place when a liturgical assembly makes music. From each field I have drawn a set of theories that help us pay attention to various dimensions of that action, and to interpret what we see, hear, and experience in particular ways. Taken together, they provide the basis for an integrated approach to research procedures and interpretive strategies that we will explore in subsequent chapters.

These theories invite us to reflect on our assumptions about music and liturgical action, to identify particular biases, and to incorporate new perspectives. I offer them as starting points for further exploring the resources of each discipline that might inform our research and interpretive processes. Theories never remain static when we engage the lived practice of particular communities. Rather, they blend with the indigenous theories held by members of the community that become evident to us over time. In studying the musical performance of a worshiping assembly, we discover implicit patterns of interpretation that reshape our theories and reformulate our assumptions.

Theories are always interpretations of practice. Yet the relationship of theory and practice functions differently in each of the three disciplines we will explore. Liturgical scholars assume the churches' ongoing, lived experience of worship as the basis for their work. Yet much of our theoretical and theological discourse is based on general patterns of practice, and in some measure is influenced by the unacknowledged contexts that have shaped the experience and assumptions of individual scholars.[1] Ethnomusicology and ritual studies, on the other hand, focus more specifically on the empirical study of lived practice, both musical and ritual, drawing theories more directly from the performing traditions of specific communities. For this reason, an integration of perspectives and field research methods from these two disciplines can provide liturgical scholars with a richer base for accessing the churches' lived practice.

We note also that liturgical studies is distinguished from these other disciplines in that theoretical and theological discourse function side by side within the field. Liturgical theology, which makes certain truth claims about the meanings mediated in liturgical practice, is a specific discourse within the comprehensive field of liturgical studies. Since the intent of the discipline as a whole is to increase understanding of how the churches' traditions of prayer are avenues of encounter between the living God and the ecclesial body, it is not surprising that liturgical theory moves easily in and out of theological discourse. This movement from theoretical to theological discourse will be reflected in the orientations I draw from liturgical studies.

Orientations from Liturgical Studies

There has been a considerable development in liturgical understandings over the past several decades. I highlight three areas of development that set the stage for the particular orientations explored in this section. First, liturgical historians, whose earlier work had focused primarily on finding a single common origin of Christian worship patterns, now stress the essential pluriformity of Christian liturgy, both in its origins and in its historical evolution.[2] At the time of Vatican II and comparable moments in other denominations, these historians reawakened our liturgical imagination to liturgical diversity, and in so doing, helped usher in a period of liturgical renewal and creativity. Second, the contemporary focus on inculturation, and

---

[1] For reflections on the interplay of theory and practice see, for example, Michael B. Aune, "Ritual Practice: Into the World, Into Each Human Heart," *Inside Out: Worship in an Age of Mission,* ed. Thomas H. Schattauer (Minneapolis: Fortress Press, 1999) 151–79.

[2] See Paul F. Bradshaw, *The Search for the Origins of Christian Worship: Sources and Methods for the Study of Early Liturgy* (New York: Oxford University Press, 1992). These shifting views of liturgical historians underscore the truth that all history is interpretive of the experience for which it accounts.

more specifically on liturgical inculturation, underscores that liturgical diversity is not only characteristic of our past but also necessary and desirable for the future of Christian liturgy.[3] Theories of liturgical inculturation reflect a significant shift in how the churches regard culture, underscoring the essential role of culture in Christian faith and ritual practice.[4] Third, a move away from text-based methods of analysis to a broader incorporation of the human and social sciences has characterized the work of numerous liturgical scholars, and in turn has shifted our theories about how meaning is mediated in liturgical performance. This move "beyond the text"[5] has refocused our attention on the complex, often nonverbal domains of liturgical action through which theological meaning is made and appropriated.

These shifting perspectives in the field of liturgical studies have affected what scholars assume about the nature of Christian liturgical performance, about its pluriform and culturally-mediated expressions, and about the role of music and other expressive arts in liturgical prayer. They are reflected in the set of assumptions about liturgy and music we will now explore—assumptions that orient us to liturgical action and that provide starting points for our exploration of a particular community's musical-liturgical performance.

Liturgy is an act of a local church[6]—an actualization of a local *ekklesia* as ecclesial and social body in a particular time and place.[7]

---

[3] See Anscar J. Chupungco, *Liturgical Inculturation: Sacramentals, Religiosity, and Catechesis* (Collegeville: The Liturgical Press, 1992).

[4] Louis J. Luzbetak, *The Church and Culture* (Maryknoll, N.Y.: Orbis Books, 1995) 133–397.

[5] Lawrence A. Hoffman, *Beyond the Text: A Holistic Approach to Liturgy* (Bloomington: Indiana University Press, 1987); also Nathan D. Mitchell, *Liturgy and the Social Sciences* (Collegeville: The Liturgical Press, 1999).

[6] The term "local church" may have several meanings. Here, it is used to refer to a single community that shares life and worship. But it may also refer to a larger ecclesial group, such as a diocese, or to a sociocultural group of people. This last sense is often the primary referent in discussions of the construction of "local theology." See Robert J. Schreiter, *Constructing Local Theologies* (Maryknoll, N.Y.: Orbis Books, 1993).

[7] Joseph A. Komonchak, "The Local Realization of the Church," *The Reception of Vatican II*, ed. Giuseppi Albergo, Jean-Pierre Jossua, and Joseph Komonchak (Washington, D.C.: Catholic University of America Press, 1987)

Although liturgical rites are historically and socially mediated, they are always expressed locally. The practice of local assemblies is thus a primary referent, we might say a matrix, of the church's understanding of its ritual life. Within each local setting, faith and culture are inseparable. God acts in specific times and places, and through the idioms, perceptions, and insights of a people's culture. A community's response is mediated through cultural realizations and aesthetic expressions—modes of speech, dress, thought, and action—that are essential rather than incidental to the churches' worship and faith.

Worship is therefore always contextualized.[8] No matter how universal ritual patterns are thought to be, they are enacted in particular contexts, and context plays a crucial role in how they are undertaken and understood. A community's context is multidimensional—at once social, historical, cultural, political, religious, and familial. These dimensions of context are part of the very fabric of its worship. They affect how a community addresses God, how God is perceived to act, how persons relate to one another as body, and how they situate themselves in the larger world and Church.

This focus on the local gives a particular perspective to how we understand liturgical books and documents to be carriers of "the rite." Prayer books and official documents are essential tools, since they formulate perspectives, procedures, and patterns that shape local performance, and situate a particular community's worship within a larger sphere of practice. Used ritually, they function symbolically, becoming part of the meaning making that takes place. But they do not of themselves account for or describe all that takes place in local performance. The manner in which the rite has been mediated historically in a particular place is powerfully formative for how a community worships, and how it negotiates and understands its place in the larger ecclesial body.

Each local celebration of liturgy is a profoundly relational activity. In the event of public worship, a community participates actively in the relationships that identify it spiritually and eccle-

77–90; Jean Corbon, *The Wellspring of Worship*, trans. Matthew J. O'Connell (New York: Paulist Press, 1988) 80; Collins, *Worship: Renewal to Practice*, 97, 118.

[8] For reflections on context and local church see Schreiter, *Constructing Local Theologies*, 1–21.

sially[9]—relationships among members of the community, relationships with the rest of the human family, relationship with divine mystery. How these relationships are actualized and perceived varies from community to community, and from one event of worship to another. Liturgical scholars speak of liturgy as a living encounter, a fresh experience of the God of Christian faith—the triune God manifest in the person of Jesus Christ, now given over to the world and church as Spirit.[10] But how the action is experienced as the memory of Jesus, as the action of the Spirit, is uniquely mediated through the complex forms of human communication and action a community cultivates. Likewise, the manner in which relationships are actualized within the community, their quality and form, and the community's sense of corporate identity are distinct—known through the various roles that are assumed and the embodied patterns of its word and gesture. Nor is a community's worship neutral vis-à-vis the larger human community. The patterns of its ritual action become, in some measure, paradigmatic for action outside the sphere of liturgy. They shape its expectation of how God's promises for the world will be realized within concrete human social-political history, and the role that the community might play in bringing these promises to fulfillment.[11]

Local worship is thus embodied theology—a ritual encounter with the living God, present within the church-at-worship—that is at the heart of all theological activity.[12] In liturgy, local communities mediate differing ways of being in relation to God and the world, differing models of "being church," not by stating them in words but by embodying them ritually. Mary Collins points out that these perceptions of relatedness are more truthfully and reliably communicated through the ambiguous modes of nonverbal communication and action—movements, gestures, postures, ways of gathering and acting

[9] Mary Collins, *Contemplative Participation: Sacrosanctum Concilium, Twenty-five Years Later* (Collegeville: The Liturgical Press, 1990) 55.

[10] Kevin W. Irwin, *Context and Text: Method in Liturgical Theology* (Collegeville: The Liturgical Press, 1994) 46–50.

[11] Don E. Saliers, *Worship as Theology: Foretaste of Glory Divine* (Nashville: Abingdon Press, 1994) 51, 175, 183; Theodore W. Jennings Jr., "Liturgy," *The Encyclopedia of Religion,* ed. M. Eliade (New York: Macmillan, 1987) 8:582; Aidan Kavanagh, *On Liturgical Theology* (New York: Pueblo Publishing Co., 1984) 144.

[12] Kavanagh, *On Liturgical Theology,* 75.

ritually—than through the verbal domain of texts and words.[13] To understand how worship is theological, therefore, we must explore the human bodiliness through which it is expressed. We must acknowledge that human gestures of eating, drinking, and proclamation—foundational ways in which Christian communities express a fullness of communion with God and among participants—are at the heart of a whole range of bodily expression through which a community articulates its spiritual and ecclesial identity. The particular gestures and postures cultivated by a community articulate and encode meanings.[14] They reflect and cultivate attitudes, ways of being in the world, that in turn permeate the intellectual, social, and spiritual lives of those engaged, and give rise to perceptions of both self and Church.

Within this embodied ritual, faith is emergent. Liturgical assemblies are "likely to anticipate new themes and attempt new syntheses" that will subsequently be systematized in theological discourse.[15] For this reason, those who study liturgical performance need to attend to the new intuitions of God's action in the world that may emerge in practice. They will need to be attentive not only to what confirms expected patterns, but to what subverts them; not only to what is harmonious with current theological explanations of worship, but to what is discordant.

One point of emphasis in current understandings of Christian worship is the role of the whole assembly as subject of the liturgical action.[16] Although numerous and varied forms of leadership are taken—roles understood to be important, even essential, to the action—it is the assembly as a whole, as embodied presence of Christ,

[13] Collins, *Worship*, 73–90.

[14] Ronald Grimes, "Liturgical Supinity, Liturgical Erectitude: On the Embodiment of Ritual Authority," *Studia Liturgica* 23:1 (1993) 51.

[15] Collins, *Worship*, 95, 131.

[16] Margaret Mary Kelleher, "Ritual Studies and the Eucharist: Paying Attention to Performance," *Eucharist: Toward the Third Millennium* (Chicago: Liturgy Training Publications, 1997) 52; Joyce Ann Zimmerman, "Liturgical Assembly: Who Is the Subject of the Liturgy?" *Liturgy and Music: Lifetime Learning,* ed. Robin A. Leaver and Joyce Ann Zimmerman (Collegeville: The Liturgical Press, 1998) 38–59; Yves M. J. Congar, "L'Ecclesia ou communauté chrétienne, sujet intégral de l'action liturgique," *La Liturgie aprés Vatican II*, ed. J. P. Jossua and Y. Congar (Paris: Cerf, 1967) 241; Gordon W. Lathrop, *Holy People: A Liturgical Ecclesiology* (Minneapolis: Fortress Press, 1999) 19–48.

head and members, that is the primary actor, the primary agent of the transaction. For this reason, all of a community's action—not only those patterns considered strictly "liturgical"—and all the actors must be included in any interpretation of the worship. The form the social body takes when it gathers, the modes of communication it cultivates, how persons move, how they dress, their cultural forms of expressiveness, their choices to participate or to resist participation—these are central to how members situate themselves in the body and become part of its action. They are also part of how meaning is made in worship. Meaning is not simply resident in the actions a community shares with the larger tradition—proclamation of Scriptures, preaching, actions with bread and wine, oil and water. Rather, meanings emerge through engagement and are affected by human intentionality and decision, by choices and restrictions made on choice.[17]

Because persons acting in community are the subject of liturgical action, they are also its first interpreters. Members of a worshiping community are capacitated by the Holy Spirit in baptism to speak to and about God, that is, to theologize. This capacity is honed and developed over time through faithful practice, through exposure to the mystery of saving relationships.[18] Their liturgical action gives rise to a process that is at once reflective and critical—a process that is itself theological.[19] Yet it is expressed in a language that differs considerably from the discourse used by professional theologians. It is experiential, far less concerned with precision than with identifying the human qualities of what has been touched, felt, heard, and tasted.

Liturgical events are complex actions, complex forms of human expressiveness. In worship, a community uses various modes of communication and interaction to enact the ritual—movements, sound, gestures, speech, musical idioms, objects, dress, time, space, light, and color. These complex forms of communication, sometimes referred to as the "languages" of ritual action, coalesce in a total expressive system, where they may complement each other or where

[17] Collins, *Worship*, 121–31.

[18] Mary Collins, "An Adventuresome Hypothesis: Women as Authors of Liturgical Change," *Proceedings of the North American Academy of Liturgy* (1993) 48.

[19] Kavanagh, *On Liturgical Theology*, 73–95.

they may negate, even contradict, each other.[20] They may be similar or differing "narratives" the community tells itself about itself, about how it is situated in the world, and about how God is present and active in the gathering.[21] Therefore, these various modes of communication require careful attention, since they act simultaneously and forcefully in how a community makes meaning.

Music and the expressive arts can be extremely important in shaping the whole continuum of liturgical action. These aesthetic media are carriers of cultural meaning in themselves. They are a compendium of religious, social, and cultural realizations of relatedness. From the perspective of liturgical theory, they are not embellishments but constitutive of what takes place in liturgy, affecting how all other elements are experienced and participating in the creation of meaning that takes place.[22] As we will see more fully in the next section, music and liturgical song are key modes of ritual expressiveness. Music structures time in particular ways. Song inhabits acoustical space, and singing allows particular words to take on the cultural resonances and style of a community. Music affects the whole aural character of liturgy—its rhythm, pitch, intensity, and tone—and is "powerfully formative of our embodied theology."[23] Therefore, the interpretation of an assembly's liturgy requires careful attention to the musical idioms used, to their power to take on "affecting presence"[24] for those who engage them, and to how they affect all other aspects of the liturgical action.

Orientations from Ethnomusicology

What is music? Ethnomusicologists answer this question in varied ways. John Blacking speaks of music as "humanly organized

---

[20] Peter E. Fink, *Praying the Sacraments* (Washington, D.C.: Pastoral Press, 1991) 29–44; Saliers, *Worship as Theology,* 156–66; Collins, *Worship,* 100–1.

[21] See Gaetano R. Lotrecchiano, "Ethnomusicology and the Study of Musical Change: An Introduction and Departure for Ethnoliturgiology," *Liturgical Ministry* 6 (Summer 1997) 118.

[22] Irwin, *Context and Text,* 220. See also Edward Foley, "Toward a Sound Theology," *Ritual Music: Studies in Liturgical Musicology* (Beltsville, Md.: Pastoral Press, 1995) 107–26.

[23] Saliers, *Worship as Theology,* 162.

[24] Term taken from Robert Plant Armstrong, *The Affecting Presence: An Essay in Humanistic Anthropology* (Urbana: University of Illinois Press, 1971).

sound."[25] Regula Qureshi describes music as a "system of sound communication with a social use and a cultural context."[26] Anthony Seeger speaks of music as "a system of communication involving structured sounds produced by members of a community to communicate with other members."[27] Together, these ethnomusicologists underscore that music is a form of communication—along with language, dance, and other media—that is inseparable from the human persons who make it and their cultural context.

Musical systems are distinctive ways in which human, cultural communities make meaning. Through music, human communities discover their situatedness in the world and express in unique ways the social, cultural, emotional, and spiritual condition of being human.[28] Western music is one of many cultural musical systems. Each system has its own complexity, each contains its own internal distinctions of styles and idioms. Those of us trained in the Western musical system may resist perceiving our system and its aesthetic standards as relative, but indeed this is the case. Each cultural musical system must be understood on its own terms, with its unique aesthetic preferences and its own internal referents of meaning.[29] This is not to say that musical systems exist in isolation from each other. In this time of globalization, musical systems are often juxtaposed and mutually influential. But even these processes of musical change need to be understood from within each musical system and its cultural context.

Ethnomusicologists study music in context. They assume that context is an essential part of how music comes to have meaning for a community, and why music is made in particular ways. In the perspectives that follow, I draw specifically on the work of several scholars who study music in ritual contexts. Their work orients us to the integral relationship between music making and its ritual

[25] John Blacking, *How Musical Is Man?* (Seattle: University of Washington Press, 1973) 3–31.

[26] Regula Burckhardt Qureshi, "Musical Sound and Contextual Input: A Performance Model for Musical Analysis," *Ethnomusicology* 31:1 (1987) 57.

[27] Anthony Seeger, "Ethnography of Music," *Ethnomusicology: An Introduction,* ed. Helen Myers (New York: W. W. Norton and Co., Inc., 1992) 89.

[28] Lotrecchiano, "Ethnomusicology and the Study of Musical Change," 116. Lotrecchiano gives an extended introduction to the field of ethnomusicology from the point of view of its usefulness to liturgical studies.

[29] Ibid., 119.

context, and invites to us to explore the multiple levels of meaning making that take place musically in ritual events.

* * *

Music is human action—something people do, something people make.[30] To access music in ritual contexts, we need to begin with the act of music itself, in all its complexity. Alan Merriam proposes that music involves not only sound and the evaluation of sound, but also the broad range of human behavior involved in making music and the conceptualizations people have about their music.[31] Each of these dimensions—sound, behavior, conceptualization—can be separated for analysis. But the performative nature of the musical action requires that they be understood as integrally related. In many cultures, the integral connection between the behavior involved in making music and the sound itself is clear: music and movement are inseparable activities. In these settings, to make music is to dance, to move.[32] Western music, in contrast, has focused primarily on sound itself, minimizing the inherent bodiliness of any musical communication.[33] This tendency is reinforced by our familiarity with radios and stereo systems that produce sounds without apparent human agency. But, as Anthony Seeger points out, this is an "auditory illusion" and not a feature of music.[34] All aspects of music—sound, behavior, and understanding—are important for the interpretation of music in ritual events. The particular ways participants engage in music making, the bodily ways they give it expres-

[30] Christopher Small, noting that "music is not primarily a thing or a collection of things but an activity in which we engage," goes on to identify the bias of the English language, which has no true verb for musical activity. We say "to dance" but never "to music." See *Music of the Common Tongue* (New York: Riverrun Press, 1987) 50.

[31] Alan Merriam, *The Anthropology of Music* (Evanston, Ill.: Northwestern University Press, 1964) 32. Merriam's "model" has become a primary paradigm in the field of ethnomusicology.

[32] Olly Wilson, "The Association of Movement and Music as a Manifestation of a Black Conceptual Approach to Music Making," *More than Dancing*, ed. Irene V. Jackson (Westport, Conn.: Greenwood Press, 1985) 9–23.

[33] See Susan McClary, *Feminine Endings* (Minneapolis: University of Minnesota Press, 1991) 136.

[34] Seeger, "Ethnography of Music," 89.

sion, interact with all other aspects of their ritual behavior. The musical sound they cultivate intersects other modes of communication that are operative. And people's understandings of music affect and interact with how they image the goal of the ritual action.

Timothy Rice has expanded Merriam's threefold model to identify the formative processes involved in how particular communities come to create, use, and experience music in particular ways.[35] He contends that these formative processes are at once historical, social, and individual. Music making, like ritual action, is situated in a historical tradition that has been constructed over time through processes of continuity and change. Understanding a musical event requires a twofold familiarity: first, an awareness of the evolution of performances that have shaped the community's "local tradition"; second, a familiarity with the historical development of the larger musical tradition within which it is situated. In ritual events, this historical process continues, as forms and aesthetic expressions of the tradition are shaped and re-created in the present.

Social processes affect a community's music in a similar way. Choices about musical idioms and repertoire, decisions about why particular patterns of musical performance are maintained or altered, are related to the dynamics of leadership and musical authority within the community. Likewise, they are affected by the musical expectations and preferences of other members of the group. Within these social processes, personal processes of musical formation and individual creativity take on particular importance. Formal musical training or informal modes of musical formation shape the ways in which individuals participate in making music, and the musical roles they expect to take. Personal formation affects the emotional, physical, spiritual, and multi-sensory experience that is mediated through the music, as well as particular ways a person organizes musical experience and associates it with other aspects of human life. If we wish to understand and interpret a community's current musical practice, it is essential that we understand how these three formative processes—historical, social, and personal—have shaped its patterns and choices.

Rice's orientation to process can likewise be helpful in exploring the music of a single ritual event. Liturgical music is often approached as product—a particular set of songs or pieces, items of music that can

<hr>

[35] Timothy Rice, "Toward the Remodeling of Ethnomusicology," *Ethnomusicology* 31:3 (1987) 469–88. What follows is taken primarily from this source.

be analyzed according to the musical components of form, scale, rhythm, and melodic intervals. Ruth Stone proposes an alternate perspective, stating that music is better approached within the ebb and flow of performance communication.[36] Music unfolds temporally, and its acoustic qualities—melody, rhythm, harmony, dynamics—are shaped in performance by the intentionality and expectations of those engaged. This "shaping" draws on participants' understandings of how particular styles of performance are related to the ritual context and to the occasion. It is influenced by how these understandings are expressed through musical and extra-musical behavior.[37] Musical shaping is especially evident in contexts where improvisation is assumed to be integral to musical performance. But in more subtle ways, it is operative in all music. A single piece of music performed by two ritual assemblies may vary considerably in its performative qualities. Yet the difference experienced in the performance communication is far from evident in the composed score.

Music making is inherently social. The processes of communication that take place in musical performance are themselves forms of social action and interaction.[38] Through these processes, certain types of social relationships are brought into being and expressed—relationships among those making sound by singing or performing instrumentally; relationships between performers and those who listen or who participate actively through other forms of behavior such as clapping or bodily movement.[39] This experience is a form of social bonding. Alfred Schutz proposes that music making is actually an archetype of the communicative process that underlies all social relationships—a "mutual tuning-in relationship" on which all

---

[36] Ruth M. Stone, *Let the Inside Be Sweet: The Interpretation of Music Event Among the Kpelle of Liberia* (Bloomington: Indiana University Press, 1982) 19.

[37] Gerard Béhague, introduction to *Performance Practice: Ethnomusicological Perspectives*, ed. Gerard Béhague (Westport, Conn.: Greenwood Press, 1984) 7–8; Stone, *Let the Inside Be Sweet*, 18–19; Qureshi, "Musical Sound and Contextual Input," 63.

[38] See J. H. Kwabena Nketia, "Musical Interaction in Ritual Events," *Music and the Experience of God*, ed. Mary Collins, David Power, and Mellonee Burnim (Edinburgh: T. & T. Clark, 1989) 111–24.

[39] See Stone, *Let the Inside Be Sweet*, 8–9; Anthony Seeger, *Why Suya Sing: A Musical Anthropology of an Amazonian People* (Cambridge: Cambridge University Press, 1987) 82–3; Christopher Small, *Musicking: The Meanings of Performing and Listening* (Hanover, N.H.: University Press of New England, 1998) 13.

other communication is based.[40] Musical communication makes it possible, he contends, for the "I" and the "thou" to be experienced as mutually present, as a "we."

In ritual events, then, music making is a way in which a community expresses and actualizes itself as a social body. The particular forms of relationship brought into being and maintained in the musical process affect the manner in which the community knows itself as a whole. For this reason, music in Christian ritual can have a powerful impact on how a community perceives itself as an ecclesial body.

Musical communication is multichanneled, involving not only the audio-acoustic dimensions of communication, but the visual, kinetic, and tactile modes as well.[41] Through these various channels music affects human beings as total persons, creating resonance in body and spirit, evoking affectivity, imagination, associations, and memory. As noted before, some musical traditions and ritual communities give priority to the audio-acoustic channel, interpreting the musical communication from the vantage point of sound alone.[42] Others assume an inherent connection between sound and all other dimensions of musical communication. In these traditions, kinetic modes of movement and dance, modes of visual communication and dress, are all inseparable dimensions of "the music."[43] In any ritual situation, it is important to assess which channels are cultivated and why, and then to determine the extent to which this reflects the musical tradition itself, and in what ways it flows from choices that are operative within the community. Restriction or suppression of certain channels, especially the kinetic or tactile, may be important clues to what is being communicated ritually and may indicate a community's perception of religious and spiritual reality.

Musical communication is integrally related to other modes of sound communication in the ritual context. Together they form a

[40] Alfred Schutz, "Making Music Together: A Study in Social Relationship," *Social Research* 18:1 (1951) 76, as quoted by John Blacking, "The Biology of Music-Making," *Ethnomusicology: An Introduction,* 313.

[41] Stone, *Let the Inside Be Sweet,* 7–8.

[42] This understanding of "sound" is inclusive of texts and non-texted musical sound.

[43] See John Miller Chernoff, *African Rhythm and African Sensibility* (Chicago: University of Chicago Press, 1979); Mellonee Burnim, "Black Gospel Music Tradition: A Complex of Ideology, Aesthetic and Behavior," *More than Dancing,* ed. Irene V. Jackson (Westport, Conn.: Greenwood Press, 1985) 147–67.

continuum that may include a complex set of verbal and vocal forms—speaking, preaching, chanting, calling out, reciting, moaning, shouting, or humming.[44] This sound continuum is also affected by a variety of instrumental sounds that may be melodic, harmonic, or percussive, including percussive sounds that are made bodily, such as clapping or foot tapping. Understanding what is being communicated musically requires that we pay attention to how these various aspects of sound communication interact and affect each other—creating resonance or dissonance. In some traditions, modes of musical or ecstatic speech, words of testimony, or non-linguistic vocal sounds may be considered integral to the music itself, and need to be included in any description or analysis of "the music."

Song texts are a significant part of the sound communication, especially in Christian ritual. They first require attention on their own terms, as poetic, religious, and cultural expressions embedded in particular musical expressions that are either written or oral. In performance, however, song texts are inseparable from the whole communicative event. Images of God, of community, of the human family, of God's present and future action are evoked not only by texts but by all aspects of the communication: gestural, sonic, and relational. Textual images are affected by the associations and memories that are awakened by the various channels of communication operative, kinetic and visual as well as audio-acoustic. Metaphors/images of persons and the community found in song texts may resonate with, or be in conflict with, what is experienced in other aspects of the ritual-musical event. For example, images of an inclusive social body communicated textually may be in conflict with the actual social relationships that are created and imaged in the musical or ritual action. In ritual, song texts are inseparable from all other aspects of the social, cultural, and religious communication that takes place musically, and from the interactive human strategies that are at work musically and ritually.

Music can express and evoke understandings that are related to other spheres of human life and activity: religious, social, political, and economic.[45] In religious ritual, participants often perceive music's

---

[44] See Seeger, *Why Suya Sing*.

[45] John Blacking, "Movement, Dance, Music and the Venda Girl's Initiation Cycle," *Society and the Dance: The Social Anthropology of Process and Performance*, ed. Paul Spencer (Cambridge: Cambridge University Press, 1985) 65.

effect in terms other than musical—as spiritual, aesthetic, or emotional. Music making may evoke a sense of the "presence" of supernatural beings—of God, of Christ, of the Spirit, or of ancestors—or it may communicate intimations of "Godliness," "holiness," or the action of the Spirit. The musical action may be understood as a means of interacting with these beings, offering praise, thanksgiving, intercession, or as a way of listening to their communication through word or action; of receiving power, love, or nourishment.[46] These perceptions are integral to any interpretation of music in ritual events, and account in some measure for how the ritual event has, or does not have, "affecting presence" for those engaged in the action.[47] Beyond the specifically religious or spiritual qualities perceived in the musical communication, music evokes values and emotions related to many spheres of human life. These dimensions may seldom be brought to consciousness, but they affect how a community's sense of identity is mediated in the musical-ritual action. For example, the styles and idioms of music used ritually, as well as choices about how they will be performed, communicate messages about the social, cultural, and economic situatedness of the community as a whole or of groups within it.

The aspects of musical communication explored here are all part of how meaning is made in musical-ritual events. To understand this, we must identify both the musical and social factors at work. First, musical performance itself has an emergent quality, since each performance of any music is unique.[48] This emergent quality resides in the interplay of several factors: the communicative resources of those involved; the individual competence of various musicians, especially those who take central roles of musical leadership; the goals and expectations of all the participants in the musical event; and, finally, the particular context within which the music is performed.[49] Second, human groups exist in action, and meanings arise within a group through social interaction[50]—in this case, through the performance communication. This basic sociological perspective

[46] Nketia, "Musical Interaction in Ritual Events," 112–7.

[47] See Armstrong, *The Affecting Presence*, 3–33, on "affecting presence."

[48] Béhague, *Performance Practice*, 6.

[49] Richard Bauman, "Verbal Art as Performance," *American Anthropologist* 77 (1975) 301, as quoted in Béhague, *Performance Practice*, 6.

[50] See Herbert Blumer, *Symbolic Interactionism: Perspective and Method* (Englewood Cliffs, N.J.: Prentice Hall, 1969); Stone, *Let the Inside Be Sweet*, 8, 26, 28.

underscores that musical meanings are neither fixed nor unchanging. Rather, meanings are constructed in the musical event itself and are directly related to the interpretative processes at work in the participants.[51] In music as in ritual, interpretation and meaning making involve a confluence of several factors: the past personal and cultural experience of those engaged, the perceived relevance of the music to their present situation, their anticipated response, and all other aspects of the ritual context itself. Differing meanings will emerge for various participants. Philip Bohlman points out that music has a particularly powerful capacity to embody differing meanings because of its complex forms of signification.[52] The meanings created in musical performance may be more a kind of "knowing," at once bodily and intuitive, than meaning in any objective sense.[53] In fact, the interpretive processes used by participants may not be totally conscious or active, but habituated—meanings taken for granted. But always, meanings are created and re-created through shared musical action, and are never totally separable from that context or from the persons involved in the music making.[54]

Orientations from Ritual Studies

Theories of ritual developed in the fields of anthropology and ritual studies have been in considerable flux in the last few decades. In his recent essay *Liturgy and the Social Sciences*, Nathan Mitchell offers a perspective on this evolution and its impact on several Christian liturgical scholars.[55] He demonstrates the gradual emergence of a "classic paradigm," one in which ritual was understood

---

[51] Béhague, *Performance Practice*, 7–8; Stone, *Let the Inside Be Sweet*, 8. Here I have integrated several images from Stone's work.

[52] Philip Bohlman, "World Musics and World Religions: Whose World?" *Enchanting Powers: Music in the World's Religions*, ed. Lawrence E. Sullivan (Cambridge, Mass.: Harvard University Press, 1997) 72.

[53] Blacking, "Movement, Dance, Music and the Venda Girl's Initiation Cycle," 65. See also Rebecca J. Slough, "'Let Every Tongue, by Art Refined, Mingle Its Softest Notes with Mine': An Exploration of Hymn-Singing Events and Dimensions of Knowing," *Religious and Social Ritual: Interdisciplinary Explorations*, ed. Michael B. Aune and Valerie De Martinis (Albany: State University of New York Press, 1996) 175–208.

[54] Stone, *Let the Inside Be Sweet*, 25.

[55] Summary drawn from Mitchell, *Liturgy and the Social Sciences*.

to be a carrier of social meaning—at once symbolic, enduring, invariable, and ultimately independent of those who engage in it. In this model, meanings, encoded in rites, lie beyond the power of participants to manipulate or control them. While some local meanings may emerge in ritual performance, the most stabile meanings are those authoritatively encoded in its invariable and repeatable patterns. Mitchell goes on to demonstrate how recent theorists of ritual seriously challenge this "classic" paradigm. Their theories offer liturgists alternative ways of interpreting ritual and the processes by which meaning is made within ritual events.

The orientations from ritual studies used here draw primarily on the work of Catherine Bell, Ronald Grimes, and Theodore Jennings. Grimes proposes that ritual is not a "what," a thing, but a "how"—that is, a quality of human action, a way of doing things.[56] Bell maintains, similarly, that ritual is not a single universal category of human activity that can be defined and analyzed apart from other forms of human action.[57] Rather, ritual is a strategic and flexible way of acting, situated within the social processes and the cultural predilections of the communities who ritualize. These orientations focus us on the particularity of a community's performance, inviting us to explore how meaning is mediated within the action itself. They enable us to explore the operative ecclesiology of a worshiping community, and the "operational efficacy"[58] of liturgical rites—the reasons why communities cultivate them in specific ways, and the social and spiritual experience they effect in particular settings.

* * *

Classically, ritual has been perceived as a "given"—a set of prior beliefs to be symbolically enacted so that they can be reaffirmed and inculcated; or a set of actions authorized by history, by a tradition, or by "the sacred." Quite in contrast, Catherine Bell proposes that ritual action is situated and contextualized behavior. The "rite," the

---

[56] Ronald Grimes, *Ritual Criticism* (Columbia: University of South Carolina Press, 1990) 13–14.

[57] Catherine Bell, *Ritual Theory, Ritual Practice* (New York: Oxford University Press, 1992) 67–93; idem., *Ritual: Perspectives and Dimensions* (New York: Oxford University Press, 1997) 138.

[58] Meyerhoff and Moore, *Secular Ritual,* 10–15.

patterns of action drawn from the larger tradition, provide a community with a recognizable framework. But the action itself is situated in the unique ways community members act in the everyday world. Participants draw on these patterns of action. At the same time, they distinguish and privilege their ritual action through particular strategies that afford ritual a certain power and importance, that designate it as a "transaction of consequence."[59] The ritualization is likewise situated vis-à-vis the liturgical "tradition" of the people of the community, who draw on its patterns, yet distinguish their performance by the particular way they perform the rite.[60] In addition, the action is contextualized by the cultural sensitivities, the aesthetic predilections, and the cultural resourcefulness of the community.[61] Both the patterns of relationship cultivated by the community and the cultural logic by which persons know themselves to be in relationship are dynamic factors in shaping their liturgical performance.

Ritual often carries a sense of "being a certain way"[62]—of existing as objective entity, of having a life of its own. Thus it appears that what people do in a ritual event is the most natural thing possible. They are simply responding to the time, the place, and the tradition with appropriate ways of acting. What is masked by this apparent objectivity is that an acting community is in fact redefining and creating the place, the events, the tradition within which they act. They are constructing a ritual environment—a social event existing in time and space—by the very way they engage in the action.[63] Within this ritual environment, participants are able to discover

---

[59] The expression is taken from Burton Mack, "Introduction: Religion and Ritual," *Violent Origins,* ed. Robert G. Hamerton-Kelly (Stanford, Calif.: Stanford University Press, 1987) 59. See Bell, *Ritual Theory, Ritual Practice,* 88–93.

[60] Bell, *Ritual Theory, Ritual Practice,* 118–24. Bell notes, for example, that Christian Eucharist, while drawing on patterns of shared meals, distinguishes itself by the type and quantity of food, the frequency with which it is celebrated, and so forth.

[61] See Ronald A. Delattre, "Ritual Resourcefulness and Cultural Pluralism," *Soundings* 61 (1978) 281–301.

[62] Bell, *Ritual Theory, Ritual Practice,* 108–17. The images that follow come from this source.

[63] Bell, *Ritual Theory, Ritual Practice,* 98–101; idem., *Ritual,* 139.

"who they are and 'how it is' with the world."[64] Through ritual action, participants create and reappropriate a certain order of existence—personal, social, and cosmic—within which they are able to act with a relative sense of empowerment.[65] What makes the ritual effective, therefore, is not something external to their ways of acting, but is mediated and negotiated through the action itself.

To understand how this works in a particular ritual context, we must pay attention to what is done, how it is done, and by whom.[66] The entire community effects the action; all participants are agents of the ritualization. Strategies are set in motion and nuanced by the way things are done—by the expressive style, the quality, the timbre, the tone, the manner in which people act and communicate. Certain relational schemes are orchestrated through the way participants and leaders interact ritually through voice, gesture, posture, and how they locate themselves in the ritual space. Our attention to all of these modes of action is essential, since what is communicated by the ritual is created more through ambiguous modes of action than through explicit discourse.

The human body is central to this process—the body understood not only as the physical body, but as mind-body complex, as the socially situated person.[67] This is because the body functions as the point of coordination of all levels of experience—social, bodily, spiritual, and cosmological. In ritual, the body "minds itself." The strategies of the action are more corporeal than cerebral. They are embodied through postures and ways of moving in space; through styles of dress and gesture; through timbres of speech and song; through the rhythms and pulse of the action; through the range of expressive behavior used; through the bodily ways persons interact or resist interaction. They are mediated through the way persons are arranged in space; through the manner in which roles are assumed; through distinctions made by who speaks or sings and who doesn't; through

[64] Theodore W. Jennings, "On Ritual Knowledge," *Journal of Religion* 62:2 (1982) 113.

[65] Bell, *Ritual Theory, Ritual Practice*, 115; Jennings, "On Ritual Knowledge," 112, 113.

[66] See Bell, *Ritual Theory, Ritual Practice*, 94–117; also Ronald Grimes's exploration of the "ritual field" in *Beginnings in Ritual Studies*, 24–39.

[67] This material on the body is drawn from Bell, *Ritual Theory, Ritual Practice*, 94–117, and Jennings, "On Ritual Knowledge," 115.

the use of time; through the strategies of who controls the timing of the action. Relational schemes are known by "embodying" them in the course of the ritual action.

Formality, fixity, repetition, and invariance are qualities that some assume to be intrinsic to ritual.[68] Yet Bell points out that these qualities are actually strategies a community may use to embody its action. Informality, improvisation, and variability may likewise characterize the community's ritual. The particular strategies employed affect the manner in which persons experience themselves to be related. They communicate sociocultural messages about how this community is "ordered" and about how sources of power are distributed and operative within the community.

An example, taken from Bell, serves to illustrate. Formalism may come to dominate a community's ritual. This quality of action is often communicated through the use of a restricted code of speech and behavior, one in which speech is more conventional than personally expressive. Gestures used in a formal situation are often fewer in number, more restrained or prescribed, than in informal settings. Ritual leaders may use styles of oratory that differ from everyday speech—limited vocabulary, intonation, fixity of order and style. What is communicated in formalized ritual activities tends to be aesthetically powerful, endowed with beauty and grace and invoking "a metaphoric range of considerable power, a simplicity and directness, a vitality and rhythm."[69] However, it is also difficult to challenge, to question, or to disrupt. This is because formality orchestrates roles with implicit lines of authority and communicates complex messages very economically—messages about social and hierarchical relationships, about how identity is negotiated within a particular social sphere.

Formalism is only one quality that may take precedence in a ritual event. Discursiveness, traditionalizing,[70] or improvisation may be operative, or a heightening of the "performative" quality of the action, or an informality that makes use of an open rather than a restricted code of speech and behavior. Informality may be employed

[68] What follows is taken from Bell, *Ritual*, 138–70; and Bell, *Ritual Theory, Ritual Practice*, 106–17.

[69] Basil Bernstein, "A Socio-Linguistic Approach to Social Learning," *Penguin Survey of the Social Sciences*, ed. J. Gould (London: Penguin, 1965) 165, as quoted in Bell, *Ritual*, 141.

[70] See Bell, *Ritual*, 145–50.

as a means of valuing personal sincerity and intimate participation, or as a way of creating a sense of ritual change rather than stasis. Rarely is a single strategy evidenced throughout. Each community nuances the action as a unique blend of possible ways of acting ritually, creating a loosely integrated sense of whole. Together, these strategies work to create a sense of "world," a redemptive order of existence within which participants are empowered.

The process by which this happens is somewhat circular. The strategies generated by a community within the ritual environment are then reimpressed upon participants in such a way that they provide an internalized "sense of ritual," a cultivated "sixth sense" of how ritual works in ways that are effective. In turn, these internalized schemes affect participants' perception of how the world works and how they can live in the world as constructed by the ritual. As Theodore Jennings points out, this acquired "sense of ritual" is not only a way of seeing the world differently, but a way of acting differently in the world.[71]

Language plays a particular role in the ritual process and is given special precedence in Christian liturgy. Bell reminds us that in ritual, language is inseparable from the whole continuum of communication that takes place within the ritual sphere.[72] Language attempts to communicate with a certain directness and precision—most often evoking agreement or disagreement. Ritual activities, on the other hand, attempt to express what cannot be expressed through other means. They embed and embody language in more complex and ambiguous modes of expression that allow for a diversity of interpretations, which evoke both consent and resistance and allow persons to find themselves in a more fluid and flexible way within the community's action.

Texts, as a form of ritual language, require a particular kind of attention. The importance placed on texts, how texts are used and by whom, is a significant part of the ritual strategies at work. A community's emphasis on the "fixity" of texts, especially those derived from another era, tends to underscore the past as foundational for what is mediated in the ritual. Fixed texts often imply that certain

[71] Jennings, "On Ritual Knowledge," 117.

[72] See Bell's discussion of ritual and language in *Ritual Theory, Ritual Practice*, 110–4, 130–40; and *Ritual*, 139–50. See also Grimes, *Beginnings in Ritual Studies*, 32–4.

persons are their appropriate interpreters. Open texts, on the other hand—those improvised, negotiated, or reinterpreted within the action—may imply a more collective ownership and a more contemporary locus for the values mediated in the ritual.

Ultimately, Bell contends, ritual action has a particular way of aligning a community with sources of power.[73] She points out that power is not a thing, residing in particular persons or institutions. Rather, power is a relational dynamic, constructed within human interaction, and authority is negotiated within social dynamics. Each community's ritual action is a unique negotiation of power. The relative empowerment that participants come to experience in ritual is rooted in how relationships of power are at work—how authority is recognized and validated in the ritual event, but also how it is limited and constrained. These dynamics of power involve the interdependent and mutually limiting roles of ritual leaders or "specialists" (those holding office or having particular status) and others who are "nonspecialists." The authority of those who lead is validated through the many ways it is objectified in the ritual, such as dress, modes of speech, physical location, and through the consent and affirmation of other members of the community. But authority is also limited and constrained through strategies of resistance on the part of individual participants, or through the recognition that what is said or done by those in authority is disconnected from the real world and from life as experienced by others.

The fruit of this active negotiation of power is the creation of a social body that is at once diverse and fluid, a shifting network of relationships rather than a single body marked by full consensus. Both resistance and consent are essential parts of the efficacy of the action. Relationships of power negotiated within the ritual are legitimized as being "the way things are in the universe"—derived from powers and realities beyond the event, grounded in God, in the tradition, in the cosmos. Within the event, persons discover a situated sense of themselves within the relational sphere of power that is operative and evoked. Having internalized the strategies at work, they are able to act beyond the rite.

What then does ritual mean? How is meaning made in ritual events? Bell and others contend that rituals never present a single

[73] What follows is taken from Bell, *Ritual Theory, Ritual Practice*, 106–18, 130–42, 197–223.

meaning. Persons engage in ritual action precisely because the meanings expressed escape explicit discourse; they require ambiguity and diversity of interpretation. For power to be accessed, for relationships to be "redemptively reordered,"[74] for persons to discover "how the world is," "who they are in the world,"[75] and how to act in the world, embodied ritual action must always defer any final statement, any consensus about its meaning. In so doing, ritual reflects the ambiguity and plurivocality of the cosmos, whose order it attempts to reflect and access.

Conclusion: Music Making as Ritual Performance

How we conceive music's role in ritual events will affect all our modes of analysis and interpretation. Based on the threefold orientations we have just explored, we can now articulate more clearly the perspective of this method: that music making and ritualization must be interpreted as an integrated whole.[76] Music unfolds not only *in* ritual but *as* ritual, as a mode of ritual performance.[77] An assembly's musical performance inevitably influences the whole ritual process. At the same time, participants' ritual and spiritual expectations and commitments shape the parameters of musical performance. Music making can accomplish the articulated or unarticulated goals and purposes of the ritual. Music is temporal in nature, making time available to human perception.[78] Musical activity is a way a community orders and structures time, providing a temporal framework for shared experience within which the social identity of participants is constructed and available for conscious

[74] Bell, *Ritual Theory, Ritual Practice,* 114–7.

[75] Jennings, "On Ritual Knowledge," 113.

[76] See, for example, Béhague, *Performance Practice,* 7–9; and Regula Qureshi, *Sufi Music of India and Pakistan: Sound, Context and Meaning in Qawwali* (Cambridge: Cambridge University Press, 1986) 103–31, regarding the relationship between music and context.

[77] Thomasina Neely, "Belief, Ritual, and Performance in a Black Pentecostal Church: The Musical Heritage of the Church of God in Christ" (Ph.D. dissertation, Indiana University, 1993) 11–12, 36.

[78] Suzanne Langer speaks of music as "time made audible," in *Philosophy in a New Key* (New York: New American Library, 1951) 110. See also her *Feeling and Form: A Theory of Art* (New York: Charles Scribner's Sons, 1953) 104–19.

appropriation. The choice of particular styles and idioms of musical sound can situate a community's ritual experience vis-à-vis its everyday life—creating distance or closeness. Musical performance may be a way of marking or enacting a community's transition from daily life into the ritual context, and transitions within the ritual performance itself.[79] Musical styles affect how persons engage bodily in the musical-ritual process. Musical forms carry implicit ecclesiological messages about relationships within the worshiping community.[80] Music inhabits acoustic space, affecting how persons feel united or isolated within the community and the action. Music making can enable an assembly to experience itself as a unified body, while allowing for considerable diversity, even resistance.[81] Words can be expressed musically as relational gestures that transcend the verbal. Finally, music making orchestrates relationships and interactions within the community, and may be a central means of evoking the presence of spiritual beings.

---

[79] Deborah Wong and Renee T. A. Lysloff, "Threshold to the Sacred: The Overture in Thai and Javanese Ritual Performance," *Ethnomusicology* 35:3 (1991) 315–48.

[80] Edward B. Foley, "Musical Forms, Referential Meaning, and Belief," *Ritual Music*, 165.

[81] See Bohlman, "World Musics and World Religions," 71–5.

2 The Research Process

A research process is a pathway to insight and interpretation—one that flows from the nature of what it is we want to know. As stated at the outset, the purpose of the method we are considering is to provide fresh and new understandings of music as both worship and theology through a focused study of music within the ritual performance of one community. Based on the theoretical orientations of the last chapter, we are now in a position to articulate more fully what it is we want to know and what research procedures will be most appropriate for our purposes. This chapter will identify the starting points for our investigation, and then explore particular research methods and interpretive strategies that suit our goals. Many of these are drawn from the field research methods of ethnomusicology, anthropology, and ritual studies, as these provide a basis for a liturgical and theological interpretation. Finally, this chapter will propose a process by which the experience of one community's music and worship can become a source for further reflection within the field of liturgical studies or other pastoral contexts.

Starting Points for the Research

What It Is We Want to Know?

Based on the orientations of the last chapter, we can now say that to know a community's music as worship and as theology, we must come to know the music in all its performativity. That is, we must know it:

- as the action of this local community, related to all aspects of the community's context;
- as cultural communication, embedded in the community's cultural associations and spirituality;
- as revelatory of God's action;
- as relational activity, a way the community performs relationships within the social/ecclesial body; and a way the communal body as a whole is brought to expression and is articulated as a particular "model" of church;
- as acoustic-bodily-conceptual communication;
- as multidimensional and multichanneled performance— awakening certain associations, memories, intimations of "Godliness" and "holiness";
- as evoking and expressing relatedness beyond the community—to God and to others;
- as generating/making meaning within the musical performance;
- as the performance of a "local tradition"—situated within a larger musical-cultural tradition.

Within liturgy, every aspect of music's performativity is related to the action of the worship event and to all its complex dimensions. Musical performance is dynamically related to the forms of communication used. It affects and is affected by the qualities of the verbal and gestural interaction that takes place. It is integral to the manner in which roles are taken and relationships of authority and power are negotiated. It affects the way in which the spatio-temporal environment as a whole is created and nuanced by members of the community. Music is a means by which persons come to a sense of empowerment to live in the world that is mediated ritually. Musical performance is a way in which the community actualizes itself as an ecclesial body, and affects the sense of redemptively reordered relationship that flows from the sources of power a community accesses in its worship. A community's music can be known as worship as we learn the integral manner in which music shapes and is shaped by their action as a whole.

Worship and its music are performed theology precisely because they express embodied relationality—they actualize and manifest the spiritual, ecclesial, eschatological, and ecological relationships that express and create a community's identity. Theology is, after all, about relationships—the deep spiritual and ecclesial relationships that mark a religious people. These relationships, comments ethnomusicologist Christopher Small, "are enormously complex—too complex to be expressed in words. But that does not mean they are too complex for our minds to encompass. . . . [Music and ritual] provide us with a language by which we can understand and articulate these relationships."[1]

The Research Tasks

The first task of our research, then, is to come to know the music as we come to know the community—that is, as we learn the complex relationships that are mediated in the community's life and in its liturgical-musical performance. For this learning to take place, the community must be at the center of how we learn and interpret its practice. They are the subjects, the agents of their musical worship and rightfully its first interpreters. The images, understandings, and associations by which they describe and reflect on their experience need to become the categories by which we come to know and interpret it. Based on this knowledge, our second task will be to make our learnings available for further reflection within the field of liturgical studies or within the pastoral group who receives the research.

These two tasks are best accomplished through a research process that is long-term and ethnographic. Ronald Grimes has underscored the importance of long-term research. In his response to a study of Roman Catholic liturgical performance, Grimes urges a minimum of one year of investigation.[2] My own research experience suggests that a two- or three-year study provides a better framework for nuanced understandings to emerge. This longer framework is especially important when the cultural experience of the researcher(s) differs from that of the community involved.

Ethnography is a mode of interpretation, used in several of the social and human sciences, that employs descriptive and narrative writing as tools for investigation and analysis.[3] The goal of ethnography

---

[1] Small, *Musicking*, 13–14.

[2] Grimes, *Ritual Criticism*, 28–62.

[3] New images of ethnography have emerged in the field of critical anthropology. See George E. Marcus and Dick Cushman, "Ethnographies as Texts," *Annual Review of Anthropology* 11 (1982) 25–69; David J. Hess, "The New Ethnography and the Anthropology of Science and Technology," *Knowledge and Society* 9 (1992) 1–26.

is to develop sustained, detailed, and polyvocal descriptions of performance that are rooted in the understandings and categories of those who perform.[4] For our purposes, the ethnographic process is an effective way to access and describe the nuanced and embodied complexity of musical-liturgical performance—to portray "lived liturgical life."[5] It allows those engaged in the research to explore descriptively the modalities and strategies of the community's performance, the dynamic interplay between nonverbal and verbal expression, and to record the perceptive commentary given by participants. Through rich, "thick"[6] descriptions of what is done and said, the researcher(s) can portray the "event" character of performance—its flow, its timing, its multidimensionality and polytexturality—that can only partially be reduced to other forms of expression.

The Researchers

Who, then, are the appropriate persons to carry out this study? The answer lies in at least two factors: the competencies and the personal qualities needed for effective research. Musical skills are necessary if researchers are to access a community's music on its own terms. At least one of those involved must have the ability to engage, as a musician, in exploring the musical understandings of both musicians and nonspecialists alike. In addition, those engaged in the study must have a growing familiarity with the specific musical, liturgical, and cultural traditions of the community. They must know the denominational tradition within which the community's worship is situated—both the ritual books and commentaries current within the denomination, and the "performed experience" of the tradition within a spectrum of communities. Finally, they must know the field of liturgical studies or the pastoral group for whom the research is undertaken, and the particular traditions and categories of interpretation used within this field or context.

In addition to these competencies, the personal quality of empathy is essential to the research process. Those who engage in the

---

[4] See Nathan D. Mitchell's summary of new perpectives on anthropological ethnography, *Liturgy and the Social Sciences* (Collegeville: The Liturgical Press, 1999) 80–93.

[5] Grimes, *Ritual Criticism*, 50.

[6] Clifford Geertz, *The Interpretation of Cultures* (New York: Basic Books, 1973) 3–30.

study must be able to move beyond their own categories of interpretation, to see things from another point of view, and to reach an empathetic awareness of how a community makes meaning musically and ritually. Empathy as a research tool is described by one commentator as a kind of "spiritual discipline"—the ability to be with a community without judgment "until you flow with the rhythm, the pace of its action—until your interior metronome is beating with theirs."[7] This comparison of empathy in research with spiritual discipline is very useful. In the practice of contemplative prayer, for instance, one must give oneself over to the prayer experience, to the Divine, without mental judgments or observations. Only later does the one who prays reflect on the experience. Attending to the musical-liturgical expression of a community requires the same willingness to let go of preconceived ideas and models of what one will find. Only much later, after fully entering the new "cultural world," and reaching a point of compatibility with the way members of the community understand it, can the researcher reflect on and interpret what is found there.

Based on these competencies, several models for the study emerge. The research might be undertaken by a single scholar/practitioner, who has both the expertise and personal sensitivities necessary. A research team of two or three persons—persons with complementary background and expertise—might likewise engage in joint research. A third model, one formulated in the field of organizational development, could involve an "insider-outsider" research team.[8] Here, one or more members of the community being studied take an active role in the research process and in shaping its outcomes. Options two and three might be especially effective if the community studied is multicultural. They allow each member of the team to study one of the cultural community's music on its own terms, and the team together to explore the interplay of these musics in the life and worship of the parish.

No matter who is involved in the study, it is essential that the researcher(s) identify her/his social location at the outset of the research.

---

[7] Dalen Daniels, a spiritual director and retreat leader; personal conversation.

[8] This model was developed by Jean M. Bartunek and Meryl Reis Louis within the field of organizational development. See *Insider/Outsider Team Research*, Qualitative Research Methods, vol. 40 (Thousand Oaks, Calif.: Sage Publications, 1996).

Each of us is shaped by our cultural background, educational training, denominational experience, age, gender, cultivated interests, attitudes, and experience—all of which provide a lens through which we interpret our own experience and that of others. By identifying our own conditioned perspectives, we are better able to recognize how they affect our perceptions and our ability to enter fully into the world of others so as to discover and grasp what is meaningful to them.

The Communities of Accountability: The Phases of the Research

Throughout the study, the researcher(s) functions within two "communities of accountability." The first is the community/parish that agrees to participate in the research. To them, the researcher(s) is accountable for the consistency of her/his interpretations with the community's indigenous understandings of their music and worship. The second is the field of liturgical studies, or the pastoral group for whom the research is undertaken. To this second group, the researcher(s) is accountable to make accessible the learnings of the research in terms that will serve the purposes of the group.

The bridge between the two communities of accountability is the ethnographic presentation written by the researcher(s) at the end of the first phase of the research. This presentation is a candid, evocative portrait of the community's music and worship.[9] Here, the researcher(s) "speaks with" community members (rather than of or for them), describing the meaningfulness of their musical-liturgical action using their own language and categories of interpretation. Within the same presentation, the researcher(s) also addresses the academic field or pastoral group who will receive the research, exploring the significance of the community's music-worship within the categories of interpretation used within the field. Thus, the presentation initiates a second phase of the process: a collaborative exploration within the academic or pastoral field of what has been learned in the research. This second phase of the process will be the subject of Chapter 3.

I take the terms "meaningfulness" and "significance" from Fred Clothey's "Comprehensive Interpretation of Ritual."[10] Clothey assumes that meanings are always plural and multidimensional. This

---

[9] Grimes, *Ritual Criticism*, 57–8.

[10] Fred W. Clothey, "Toward a Comprehensive Interpretation of Ritual," *Journal of Ritual Studies* 2:2 (1988) 147–61. Definitions taken from 148–51.

notion resonates with the theories of meaning in music and ritual explored in Chapter 1, that meanings are dynamic, arising within social processes and interaction, and therefore are fundamentally interpersonal and social. In light of this, Clothey posits that meaning is a "unit of intelligibility," a single consideration within a whole universe of possibilities. Meaningfulness is the mosaic of meanings ascribable to a phenomenon within its total cultural setting. The meaningfulness of a community's musical and liturgical action is like a woven tapestry, "a picture of the landscape of meanings" held within the community.[11]

Significance, on the other hand, refers to the linkage between the world of a community's ritual action and the disciplinary and theoretical world of the researcher. Those who study and interpret a community's musical-ritual action first "re-weave" the fabric of meanings known by the community, and then identify the significance of these meanings in light of the interpretive framework of another field. Always, what is presented must be faithful to the indigenous landscape.

It is clear from what we have just explored that choosing a community will be crucial for what will be learned in the study. Communities must be willing to participate in the process, and, in most cases, should actively cultivate music in their worship. At this moment in our history, cultural communities whose musical idioms were formerly excluded by the aesthetic preferences of their denomination, and who are now reintegrating these musics into worship, are of special interest. In these settings, new intuitions of social and ecclesial relatedness are being released musically, new memories and associations are being generated, new strategies of liturgical performance are emerging. Research done within these communities provides liturgical scholars with a source for new perceptions of our ritual traditions, and new understandings of the embodied theology expressed in musical and liturgical performance.

Ethical Concerns and Procedures

Ethical concerns and procedures are crucial to the whole research process. Persons, their modes of music and ritual making, must be deeply respected. A community and its musicians deserve access to the goals/methods of a particular study, and must be free to participate

---

[11] Ibid., 150.

on a voluntary basis. Most academic institutions have procedures for "Informed Consent" by which persons involved in the research give formal consent, and the institution verifies that no person involved is jeopardized in any way.[12] But the researcher(s) needs to establish protocols of courtesy and etiquette with the community as well, identifying when and how audio/video recordings will be made, how people's responses will be recorded, and how permission will be obtained for use of quotations from interviews or worship events. Further, it is important that the community know how the material will be used, to whom it will be presented, and in what form.

These formal ways of ensuring that ethical standards are met need to be accompanied by human ways of honoring a community's performance. Giving copies of all recorded video/audio materials to the community for the creation of a community archive can be one means of doing this. Keeping the ethnographic process dialogic, creating patterns of mutuality and accountability, checking assumptions about performance with various persons, and allowing their multiple interpretations to influence the researcher's understandings are also essential to honoring the community's ownership of its musical-ritual performance. The community should also be given a copy of any published or unpublished manuscript in which the researcher(s) summarizes what has been learned from the community and how the learning is interpreted for another group. As noted before, all references to the Our Lady of Lourdes community in this volume, including illustrations from their worship, are used with permission.

The Research Path and Its Interpretive Strategies

Coming to know a community's life, music, and ritual is a complex process, requiring a variety of research procedures. These procedures are most often employed simultaneously rather than sequentially. I will first present some general strategies that can be used throughout

---

[12] These procedures are aligned to state and federal "Human Subjects' Codes" that ensure the protection of research participants. In my initial use of this method, the Graduate Theological Union and the University of California approved an "exempt status" for the research. This exemption allows the names of persons and communities to be disclosed, under the conditions that it represents their desires and that they give their full consent.

the research, mentioning resources that may be helpful to those undertaking the study. I will then describe two specific means of accessing and interpreting musical performance, both drawn from ethnomusicology: the ethnography of musical performance and event-centered analysis.

Intentional Participation and Recording

The researcher's regular, intentional participation in the community's worship events and other aspects of its life is essential to the whole process. I use the term "intentional participation" as an alternative to the more common term "participant-observation," in that it communicates a singleness of purpose on the part of the researcher: to participate reflectively and reflexively in the action, recognizing that observation is an integral part of participation.[13] Participant-observation may carry a more dichotomous sense, implying that one can simply "observe" without affecting the event and community one is observing. In fact, it is precisely in this matrix of participation and interaction with the community, which affects the researcher(s), the community, and the worship events themselves, that the ethnographic process begins.

Participating in worship in more than one way can help the researcher(s) perceive its many dimensions; for example, as member of the congregation for a period of time, and then as a member of the musical ensemble. Bodily engagement in various aspects of the action is a key way of learning the community's strategies of performance. In addition to participation, a systematic recording of all events (audio, at times video) can be very useful. Recordings allow the researcher(s) to reenter, in a qualified way, the dynamic process of an event, to listen again to the timbre and tone of what is said and sung, and to the spontaneous commentary that is offered by various persons. It is important to realize, however, that recordings are selective, affected by where and how the equipment is situated and activated. Audio recording is more easily negotiated and less obtrusive in the ritual situation than is video recording. Either procedure

[13] See Anthony J. Gittins, *Bread for the Journey: The Mission of Transformation and the Transformation of Mission* (Maryknoll, N.Y.: Orbis Books, 1993) 66–71, for an alternative perception of participant-observation and helpful reflections on the pastoral sensitivities necessary for this kind of engagement with a community.

will have an impact on the worship, and require the permission of the community to record.

Participation in the music ensemble, by at least one of the researchers, is crucial for learning the musical craft of the community. Mantle Hood's image of "bi-musicality," which has become a foundational concept in ethnomusicology, offers us a helpful paradigm.[14] To know the music of another community's tradition is to learn it "from the inside," through experience and even training. The manner in which this principle is applied will depend on the circumstances of the particular research project, the persons involved and their familiarity with the musical idioms of the community.

Extensions of liturgical events, both preparatory and "overflow," are important places where a researcher(s) can interact with the community. Worship is often surrounded by numerous other "rituals"—arrivals, departures, coffee-hours, parish activities, family meals and gatherings—that are sources of rich information about the patterns of relationship and interaction that are the "style" of the community. As Catherine Bell reminds us, in worship the community makes use of and contrasts these patterns so as to privilege worship as a transaction of consequence.[15] By participating in the community's social interaction outside worship events, one can better recognize distinctions community members make between liturgy and other aspects of their shared life. Music rehearsals are also key, since they in some measure combine music learning, liturgical preparation, and informal commentary. Performances by the community's musical ensemble in other contexts—churches of the same or other denomination, political demonstrations or rallies—can reveal understandings of the music that are not as evident within the worship context.

In contrast to other methods for the study of liturgical performance, the method we are exploring does not begin with a set of questions to be asked.[16] Questions can indeed provide a useful framework for systematic observation of liturgical performance.

---

[14] Mantle Hood, *The Ethnomusicologist* (New York: McGraw Hill, 1971); Helen Myers, "Ethnomusicology," *Ethnomusicology: An Introduction*, ed. Helen Myers (New York: W. W. Norton and Co., Inc., 1992) 9.

[15] Bell, *Ritual Theory, Ritual Practice*, 8–93.

[16] See Kelleher, "Liturgical Theology: A Task and a Method," 4. She speaks of constructing "a heuristic framework of questions" that shape the investigation.

However, as a framework for research they are formulated in the categories of the researcher. For our purposes, intentional and reflective participation seems a better means by which to allow questions, data, and analytical relationships to arise from, be challenged by, and remain grounded in the actual situation of the community's experience and performance.

Ethnographic Fieldnotes

Throughout the research process, ethnographic fieldnotes provide a means of recording, describing, processing, and reflecting on the community's performance and the researcher's experience of it. Robert Emerson's *Writing Ethnographic Fieldnotes* offers extensive information on the procedures involved, and is, in fact, an excellent introduction to the whole ethnographic process.[17] Fieldnotes are best written after each liturgy or other event. Although this is a laborious task, the systematic writing of fieldnotes provides a place of insight and discovery, and ultimately is a rewarding and enlightening part of the learning process. In the early stages of the research, nuanced descriptions of as much of the music-worship event as possible can help the researcher gain a comprehensive familiarity with the community's patterns, and record the "interpretive commentary" offered by community members. Paying attention to the "qualities" and strategies of the performance, to the modes of relationship that are enacted, and to the auditory-visual-postural-gestural-kinesthetic dimensions of the action will be essential. As the research progresses, focused descriptions or analyses of particular aspects of the music-ritual can be helpful.

Ongoing, Measured Interpretation

It is important to point out that description is itself an interpretive process.[18] From the outset, what the researcher(s) chooses to describe,

---

[17] For an excellent introduction to fieldnotes and the whole ethnographic process, see Robert M. Emerson, Rachael I. Fretz, and Linda I. Shaw, *Writing Ethnographic Fieldnotes* (Chicago: University of Chicago Press, 1995). I have incorporated some aspects of their presentation in what follows.

[18] See Don S. Browning's approach to description as theological in his *A Fundamental Practical Theology: Descriptive and Strategic Processes* (Minneapolis: Fortress Press, 1991).

and the categories reflected in his/her descriptions of the event and the community's action, are interpretations of what takes place. Fieldnotes are not simply a recording of the "facts" of the event, but an active process of making sense of the experience, noting what seems to be significant for the community at any moment. This requires honesty, sensitivity, and discernment on the part of the researcher(s), and a sense of the ethical dimensions of interpreting a community's experience in a way that is true to their perceptions.

Sensitivity, intuition, the ability to "get inside and feel" the musical-ritual action are therefore tools to be cultivated by a researcher, and part of the ethics of interpretation.[19] The researcher(s) can use sympathies, sensibilities, affinities, and her/his own ritually shaped modes of seeing and knowing as a medium of empathetic understanding.[20] These intuitive modes of perception can enable the researcher(s) to discover the community's "sense of ritual,"[21] that felt sense of its ambiguous modes of communication that can reveal a community's intentionality, their perceptions of relatedness to God and others in the community. However, for these sympathies to function freely, the researcher(s) must be willing to identify her/his own "positioned subjectivity"—the attitudes, theoretical or epistemological commitments that might cause her/him to "privilege one aspect of the ritual over another instead of pursuing a more perceptive and honest inquiry."[22]

Fieldnotes are a venue for self-reflection on how the process affects the researcher(s). Discovering the processes involved in how she/he learns to participate musically and ritually can be a source of insight into the community's patterns. Doubtless, a certain "disorientation" and "reorientation" will be involved as the researcher(s) tries to understand the action from a perspective other than his/her own. Anthropologists George Marcus and Michael

[19] See Michael Price, "Ritual, Meaning, and Subjectivity: Studying Ritual as Human Religions Expression," *Epoch: UCLA Journal for the History of Religions* 16 (1988) 14.

[20] Catherine Mary Bateson, *With a Daughter's Eye* (New York: Washington Square Press, 1984) 201; Michael B. Aune, "The Return of the Worshiper to Liturgical Theology: Studies of the Doctrinal and Operational Efficacy of the Church's Worship" (unpublished, 1992) 25.

[21] Grimes, *Ritual Criticism,* 49; Ronald Grimes, *Beginnings in Ritual Studies,* 23.

[22] Aune, "The Return of the Worshiper," 25.

Fisher speak about this latter process as "defamiliarization": a discovery of the relativity of the researcher(s)' assumptions and categories, and a gradual shift to more dialogic interpretive stance.[23]

Ronald Grimes points out that good field study maximizes "the tension between inside and outside points of view so that the dialectic of distancing and empathizing can take place."[24] Fieldnotes can be a good context within which to play out this tension. As the researcher(s) becomes more grounded in the community's patterns and its categories of interpretation, she/he can record, describe, and document what only an insider would see, hear, and know in the community's social, musical, and liturgical interaction. At the same time, the researcher(s) can also record what she/he notices and knows precisely because she/he is an outsider to the experience.

Interviews and Conversations

Formal interviews with individuals or small groups are a valuable means of learning how members of a community describe, reflect on, and interpret their experience. It is important that those interviewed include persons who take musical and ministerial roles as well as other members of the community. They should represent a range of age, gender, cultural background, and length of membership. A valuable source of information will come from persons no longer involved with the community but who have played a significant role in shaping its current musical or liturgical performance.

Interviewing musicians, both individually and as an ensemble, complements the researcher(s)' participation in the music as a way of coming to understand their musical craft from their perspective. The images they use to describe, analyze, and evaluate the musical performance are important interpretive categories. In my own research, for example, members of the Gospel choir made it clear to me in our first interview that their craft is "not about performance, but about a message!" This image of "message"—the communication of the Gospel message with power, vitality, and life—became pivotal in how I came to understand the performative style of lead singers, the centrality of drums to the musical communication, the

---

[23] George E. Marcus and Michael M. J. Fisher, *Anthropology as Cultural Critique: An Experimental Moment in the Human Sciences* (Chicago: University of Chicago Press, 1986) 137–64.

[24] Grimes, *Ritual Criticism*, 59.

essential role of the whole assembly in responding to/participating in the message, and why singers spoke of their art as "preaching."

James Spradley's *The Ethnographic Interview*[25] provides an extensive introduction to the interview process. Interviews, he suggests, can be a helpful context for learning the language, images, and categories by which community members understand, interpret, and critique their musical-liturgical performance. Spradley stresses that asking persons to "describe how things are done" is a more effective way of eliciting their categories of understanding than asking them to respond to a set of questions. The former strategy leaves them free to describe the musical or liturgical action without "fitting" their response to the categories presented in the questions.

Some of the descriptions/interpretations they offer may be expressed in the technical vocabulary of musical or liturgical theory. But many will be expressed through the vocabulary of action and participation, which is often experiential, affective, and intersubjective—what was felt, heard, tasted, touched. As Aidan Kavanagh points out, these experiential and affective images are central to the reflective/critical process evoked by liturgical action—a process he posits is itself theological.[26]

Informal conversations are an equally valuable source of "spontaneous commentary" and shared reflection on what takes place. Commentary offered as persons leave a ritual event or expressed over coffee afterwards are often perceptive responses, interpretations, or evaluations of what has transpired and how it has affected them. "Being" with members of the community in various settings is a necessary complement to formal interviews.

Oral, written, and pictorial information about the community's life and history are important sources for coming to know the community and its formative experiences. They can provide information about membership, about modes of community organization, and about significant events that have shaped the community's life. Oral histories by long-term members can reveal the social and personal processes involved in the evolution of the community's musical and liturgical practice. They can also offer perceptive interpretations of current practice.

[25] James P. Spradley, *The Ethnographic Interview* (New York: Holt, Rinehart, and Winston, 1979).

[26] Kavanagh, *On Liturgical Theology*, 73–95.

Researcher's Self-reflection and Collaboration

We have mentioned the interpretive nature of description and the need for reflexivity, sensitivity, and insider-outsider tension. The rigorous attention paid by the researcher(s) to her/his own process is critical for both ethical and accurate results. In this light, it is necessary that the whole research process be dialogic, cyclical, and collaborative. As the research progresses, those engaged in the study will begin to formulate hypotheses about the significance of aspects of the community's life and action. It is often helpful to be in dialogue with a small, representative group of persons, with whom observations and hypotheses can be shared and tested. Since musical performance is central to what the researcher(s) seeks to know, several musicians may be part of this group. Conversations about the researcher(s)' observations often provide new questions, perspectives, vantage points from which to explore and describe the performance.

Accessing and Interpreting Musical Performance

All of the research procedures we have explored so far create a context for the focused study of musical performance. Two techniques, both drawn from ethnomusicological practice, have proved to be especially helpful tools in my own research: the ethnography of musical performance and event-centered analysis.

Ethnography of Musical Performance

Ethnography of musical performance is a systematic examination and interpretation of music in context, in this case, within a community's life and ritual. In an excellent introduction to this procedure, Anthony Seeger speaks of the ethnography of music as a "transcription of musical events."[27] In Western practice, musical transcriptions focus on sound structures alone. In contrast, transcriptions of musical events describe the multiple dimensions of musical performance: how sounds are made and by whom; how persons conceive and appreciate them; and how they influence

---

[27] See Seeger, "Ethnography of Music," 88–109.

other individuals, groups, and social and musical processes. This ethnographic approach allows the researcher(s) to identify the "who, where, when, how, and why" of the community's musical performance on a given occasion. It also allows her/him to situate particular performances within the larger contextualizing processes that have shaped them, processes that are historical, religious, cultural, social, and individual.[28]

Like other forms of ethnography that we have discussed so far, musical ethnography is descriptive and narrative in form. It makes use of the words, phrases, categories that musicians and other members of the community use to describe their music, their musical participation, and the effect it has on them. Some of the vocabulary used may be musical, but doubtless it will include images of the emotional, aesthetic, physiological, and religious dimensions of the musical experience as well.[29] As these categories emerge in conversation or in spontaneous commentary, the interrelatedness of categories becomes more evident to the researcher(s), providing important clues to the meanings generated within the musical experience for those who participate. These categories may differ considerably from those used by the researcher(s) to describe or interpret the music. But they are important indicators of how music is understood, and why particular styles of expression are judged to be appropriate in this religious, ritual setting. In the context of Christian worship, they carry intimations of how a community perceives divine mystery and ecclesial relatedness.

Music ethnography begins with the assumption that all persons present in the worship context are part of the music making, whether they are actively participating in the creation of musical sound or not. Too easily, we perceive musical performance in terms of performers and audience, giving primary if not exclusive attention to the "musicians." Yet, both dynamically affect the performance.[30] This is especially true within ritual events, where distinctions between performers and nonperformers are somewhat fluid, and where music's affect on the liturgical event is necessarily related to the

---

[28] Ibid., 104–6; Rice, "Toward the Remodeling of Ethnomusicology," 469–88.

[29] Seeger, "Ethnography of Music," 86.

[30] See Béhague's commentary on performance practice, *Performance Practice*, 4.

strategies and understandings of all participants. Performance ethnography focuses on multiple instances of music making, even of the same musical pieces. It assumes that ritual music making is changeable, and that each performance of a piece results from a complex interplay of choices, creativity, expectations, and tacit understandings of those taking musical leadership and other community members. Given the ritual orientations of this method, researchers need to give special attention to the how and the why of musical engagement—how sound is made, vocally and gesturally, how persons participate—since these affect the relational schemes and strategies of the whole ritual event.

Event-Centered Analysis

Event-centered analysis complements the ethnographic process by enabling the researcher(s) to explore and interpret music's relationship to all other aspects of the ritual performance. This mode of analysis is based on the procedures developed by Regula Qureshi for the analysis of music in Sufi ritual events, adapted to the goals of this method.[31] It provides a flexible framework within which the researcher(s) can identify those aspects of music making most characteristic of a community's musical performance and analyze how these become an integral part of the whole ritual process.

The analysis begins with the assumption that both ritual and music are forms of action, and that both of these modes of action are composed of identifiable aspects or dimensions that give them structure, give them form. Ritual action is structured, that is, given performative form, as participants make use of time, space, words, objects, movements, gestures, and so forth. Musical action is structured, given performative form, as participants articulate sound acoustically—melody, words, pitch, rhythm—and perform the music bodily through particular cultural styles of expressiveness and behavior. Figure 1 offers a more complete identification of the structuring aspects of both ritual action and music making, allowing for others that might emerge in local practice.

---

[31] See Qureshi, "Musical Sound and Contextual Input." Qureshi's primary goal is to identify contextual input to actual sound structures in performance. My goal is to explore the complex interaction between musical and ritual processes.

Figure 1

Structuring Aspects of Ritual Action	Structuring Aspects of Music Making
• ritual participants (inclusive/roles) • ritual time (real/perceived) • ritual space (architectural/acoustic) • ritual flow (progression) • modes of embodiment (personal/social) • postures and gestures • actions with words • actions with objects • actions with sounds • movements in space • ritual occasion (specific perceptions/ expectations/associations) (others that may emerge in local practice)	• musical participants (inclusive/roles) • acoustic articulation • words (song texts/other) • form (textual/musical) • pitch (range) • dynamic (range) • rhythm • melody • layering of sound • harmony/harmonic rhythm • duration • vocal/instrumental timbre • performance style • range/modes of expressiveness • engagement of body in music making • configuration of voices/instruments (others that may emerge in local practice)

The ritual process unfolds as participants actualize these various dimensions or structuring aspects of the ritual event through their action and interaction. That is, they organize time. They orchestrate ritual roles. They perform actions with sound, with words, and with objects. Likewise, they assume particular modes of embodiment through gesture, posture, and movements in space. They shape the flow of the ritual event. And within this process, they create together a sense of the ritual occasion.

The musical process is similar. Participants actualize certain dimensions of the music through their performative action. For example, they shape the music's acoustic articulation, as words become pitch, timbre, melody, and rhythm, and as instrumental and vocal sounds interact timbrally, rhythmically, and harmonically. They shape the musical communication, as acoustic articulation is performed through bodily expressiveness. They shape the music's performative form, through choices about repetitions and omissions, about the diversity of timbres and dynamic levels used for different verses or segments of the music. Likewise, they shape the "musical body"—the community in the act of making music—as choices about who sings and who does not sing are orchestrated musically.

In sum, the structuring aspects of ritual action and music making that we have identified become musical and ritual processes within the worship event. This takes place through the agency of the whole community, acting and interacting as a body (see Figure 2).

Figure 2[32]

Worship Event
Structuring aspects of:
Ritual Action   Music Making
are operationalized as:
Ritual Process   Musical Process
through the strategies and interactive agency of all participants.

Moreover, the particular musical strategies employed by participants play an integral role in how the ritual process unfolds. Musical processes and ritual processes become one, affecting and shaping each other. Through event-centered analysis, the researcher(s) seeks to discover both the regular and serendipitous ways this takes place; for example, how the specific strategies of the musical performance structure ritual time, how they fill acoustic space and orchestrate how persons interact within the architectural space, how they mediate ritual roles and modes of communal interrelatedness, how they embody performative ritual words, how they orchestrate ritual movements, how they shape the ritual flow. Having discovered the interaction of these processes, the researcher(s) can articulate how music is constitutive and integral to the event, that is, how music can be recognized and interpreted as worship.

Ethnographic Presentation of the Research

The first phase of the research concludes with the writing of an ethnographic presentation of what has been learned by the

[32] Adapted from ibid., 64.

researcher(s). As stated earlier, this presentation is a candid, evocative portrait of the community's music and worship that can serve as a bridge between the two groups to whom the researcher(s) is accountable: the community studied and the scholarly and/or ecclesial group to whom the research will be presented. Transmitting musical-ritual knowledge and experience into verbal forms is a translation at best and requires creative modes of presentation. The researcher(s) speaks with members of the community, representing their performative action to others not familiar with their specific styles of action and their understandings. The text needs to include a rich presentation of current performance, one that reflects the community's categories of interpretation. It also needs to represent the historical processes, both religious and cultural, that have shaped the community, and the geographic, political, social, and economic context of their current lives.[33] Clearly, such prose descriptions will require new genres of liturgical writing to emerge, forms that are faithful to the complex, ambiguous modes of a community's musical-ritual action and faithful to the polyvocality of indigenous interpretations.[34] Perhaps these new forms of liturgical literature will reawaken the lost art of liturgical ethnography, initiated by Egeria in the fourth century, that has already reaped immeasurable benefits for the field of liturgical scholarship.

Anthropologists today stress the importance of ethnography that is both "dialogical" and "polyphonic";[35] that is, ethnography in which the voices of members of the community engaged in the study are clearly present. To assist this process, the musicians and community members may be consulted in the writing of a final presentation. The text itself must allow their perceptions and interpretations to be evident. The incorporation of their interpretive phraseology and the inclusion of longer excerpts from events and

[33] See Ronald Grimes, "A Catholic Liturgical Evaluation," *Ritual Criticism*, 28–62.

[34] See Emerson, Fretz, and Shaw, *Writing Ethnographic Fieldnotes*, 169–210; see also Marcus and Fisher, "Conveying Other Cultural Experience: The Person, Self, and Emotions," *Anthropology as Cultural Critique*, 45–76.

[35] Dialogic ethnography is addressed by several anthropologists. See James Clifford, "Partial Truths," *Writing Culture: The Poetics and Politics of Ethnography*, ed. James Clifford and George E. Marcus (Berkeley: University of California Press, 1986) 1–26; Marcus and Fischer, *Anthropology as Cultural Critique*, 69–70. See also Mitchell, *Liturgy and the Social Sciences*, 85–6.

interviews can allow a plurality of meanings and interpretations to be evident to a reader.

But the ethnographic presentation has a second role. In addition to portraying the community's performance and representing the voices of the community, the researcher(s) must also address the significance of the community's musical-liturgical action for another scholarly or pastoral field. She/he must make explicit and thematic how the community's experience addresses the current understandings of music as worship and theology, using the categories of interpretation operative in professional liturgical theology or pastoral reflection. In the next chapter, I will offer a framework for this portion of the presentation, based on the interpretive categories of the field of liturgical studies, that can serve as a model.

3 Creative Dialogue with Liturgical Studies

We come now to the last phase of the method, the integration of the research just described into the comprehensive work of liturgical studies or, by implication, into the pastoral frameworks of another group that receives the research. Liturgical scholars acknowledge the importance of studying liturgical performance as a source for theological and pastoral insight, and of reflecting systematically on what is learned; yet few models exist for how this latter task might be accomplished. This chapter offers a model for such exploration, a model imaged as a creative dialogue between the academic or pastoral group that receives the research and the community's musical-liturgical performance.[1] Although my focus is the field of liturgical studies, I invite readers to explore the implications of this model for pastoral frameworks such as multicultural congregational settings, dioceses, or synods.

The paradigm offered here flows from my first use of this method within an African American Catholic community. The fruit of this study indicates that communities whose styles of music and ritual expression have historically been suppressed offer significantly new insights about liturgical action, about music as a "theologizing narrative,"[2] and about the ecclesial relationships, grounded in divine

---

[1] Robert Schreiter describes a similar dialogue between "local theologies" and the Tradition. See Schreiter, *Constructing Local Theologies*, 33–5.

[2] Image taken from Lotrecchiano, "Ethnomusicology and the Study of Musical Change," 118.

mystery, that are mediated in liturgical performance. Their local performative theology can remind us of parts of the tradition we have forgotten or chosen to ignore.[3] Collaborative reflection on their experience will stretch the images, symbols, and metaphors by which we interpret Christian worship and its diverse musical expressions, and bear fruit in richer, more comprehensive understandings of the churches' corporate prayer.

The creative dialogue I envision begins with the ethnographic presentation of those engaged in the research. In Chapter 2 we identified the dual role of this presentation: first, to portray the lived experience of the community's musical-liturgical practice; second, to explore the significance of this practice for liturgical studies (or another pastoral field) by making explicit and thematic how this experience addresses current understandings of music as worship and theology. I believe this dialogue will be far richer if it moves beyond the written presentation to an actual face-to-face encounter between professional and lay theologians, a focused yet open-ended exploration of the fruit of the research.

This chapter is an example of what might be learned through such a dialogue. I will first identify the persons who might participate in the reflective process, and then offer a framework for their conversation. Throughout, I will use selected illustrations from my own research. Note, however, that these are not the richly polyphonic, concrete, and contextualized examples that characterize a full ethnography, but a culling of multiple experiences of worship and conversations with parish members which I have organized and thematized so as to place them in dialogue with current understandings of music, worship, and liturgical theology.[4] At the conclusion of the chapter, I will offer some brief reflections on the implications of this method for the future of liturgical studies, and for how new generations of scholars might be prepared for their work.

The Dialogue Partners

The purpose of the dialogue is to stretch further the interpretive processes already begun; that is, to reflect collaboratively on the

---

[3] See Schreiter, *Constructing Local Theologies,* 34.

[4] For a fuller ethnographic presentation, see McGann, "Interpreting the Ritual Role of Music in Christian Liturgical Practice," 71–214; also *A Precious Fountain* (forthcoming).

significance of what has been presented ethnographically. The scholar(s) who has engaged in the research plays the crucial role of bridge and mediator throughout the process, since she/he is both grounded in the interpretive categories of the field of liturgical studies and richly familiar with the practice of the community. He/she invites other liturgical scholars to participate, offering his/her ethnographic presentation as a basis for the conversation. This ensures that the voices and experience of the community remain central to the reflective process. A few members of the community, key musicians or pastoral leaders, might be invited to participate, thus honoring their role as both the subjects of their musical-liturgical practice and its first interpreters. A few musicians who know the broader musical tradition of the community might be present. Finally, theologians who speak from within the ethno-cultural tradition of the community need to be represented—in this case, the voices of Black theologians will be heard throughout—since they underscore and situate the interpretive theological categories that are indigenous to the community's tradition. Black theologians, for example, are likely to assume that music, narrative, and ritual are traditional forms of systematic theology within the African American tradition, and that singing, dancing, and drumming in worship are not simply stylistic elements incidental to worship but profoundly theological acts in and of themselves.

Framework for the Collaborative Reflection

Two sets of questions provide a framework for the collaborative reflection. First, what fresh insights does this community's practice offer about music as worship? In what measure do these perceptions confirm, expand, or challenge the categories by which liturgical scholars interpret the role of music in Christian worship? In my research with the Our Lady of Lourdes community, a number of rich insights emerged about how music is integral to worship, about processes of liturgical change and inculturation, about the ecclesial relationships mediated in musical performance, about liturgical aesthetics and creativity, and about how worship is "sacred time" and "sacred space." Since these insights expand the categories currently used by liturgical scholars to reflect on music as worship, I will explore them further in the next section as an indication of the kinds of learning that can emerge from other studies.

The second part of the collaboration might address these questions: What has been learned about music as theology within a particular community's music-worship practice? Insofar as music is integral to the act of worship, how does a community's embodied theology, mediated in musical performance, address current articulations of the theological character of worship? In what ways does it confirm, expand, or challenge the theological categories by which music and worship are currently interpreted within the field of liturgical theology?[5] As Mary Collins has suggested, ritual communities are likely to anticipate new themes and attempt new syntheses that are only subsequently systematized in theological discourse.[6]

This second phase of the dialogue might center on six theological dimensions of Christian worship considered by several theologians to be perennial and enduring: that worship is theological-Trinitarian, pneumatological, sacramental, biblical, ecclesiological, and eschatological. The insights of contemporary liturgical theologians regarding each of these characteristics might serve as a springboard for the exploration. Again, I will draw on examples that proved fruitful in my own study, offering illustrations from the Our Lady of Lourdes community, and proposing questions for exploring the practice of other communities.

Reflections on Music as Worship

In our initial orientations from liturgical studies, we noted that scholars speak of musical performance as integral to all that takes place in worship, affecting the whole continuum of action and the manner in which a community makes meaning within liturgical events. This is clearly borne out in the worship of the Our Lady of Lourdes community—a small, predominantly African American Catholic community in the Bayview-Hunters Point district of San Francisco, well known to others as "Lourdes."[7] Members of the

---

[5] Other categories for this reflection might be drawn from writings on the theological character of music, as summarized by Foley, "Liturgical Music: A Bibliographic Essay," 438–45.

[6] Collins, *Worship: Renewal to Practice*, 95, 131.

[7] In 1998, the parish boundaries were extended by the diocese to include a second parish of All Hallows, whose church became a "chapel" of Our Lady

community describe music as "a gift from God which allows us to worship him better"; "a way of praising God from the heart" and of "lifting him up on our praises." Singing is a way of finding "refuge and strength in the Lord"; a means of "making it through hard times." It is a source of joy and comfort, or of healing, which sustains and nourishes their lives, giving them "something to feast on all week."[8]

Throughout this assembly's liturgy, human acts and gestures that are central to worship—giving thanks and praise, hearing and proclaiming the word of God, and making intercession—are performed musically. Songs in the gospel idiom, performed by the choir, instrumentalists, and other members of the assembly, become a powerful catalyst for the community's praise, a mode of breaking open the Word, and a means by which the biblical and liturgical word are embedded in the social history of the community. Take, for example, Brenda Moore's contemporary gospel piece "Perfect Praise," performed after Communion at a Sunday liturgy. The refrain, intoned in hushed tones by the choir, piano, and drums, spirals through ascending intervals and building crescendo into a surge of jubilant praise: "O Lord, how excellent, how excellent, how excellent is your name!" evoking acclamations, even shouts, from other members of the community. "There is none like you, none like you, none like you: Jesus, excellent is your name!" Members of the community—singing, clapping, some standing, moving to the underlying rhythms—interject their own words of praise and engagement throughout: "Amen!" "Excellent!" "He's worthy!" As the song unfolds, phrases from Paul's letter to the Philippians ("Every knee shall bow, and every tongue proclaim that he is Lord . . .") are sung in rhythmic counterpoint to a brief extension of the refrain text ("In all the earth! in all the earth! in all the earth! in all the earth . . ."), issuing in a burst of praise, "Jesus, excellent!!!" and a final resurgence of the refrain: "O Lord, how excellent, how excellent, how excellent . . . ." Members of the community report that this communal and highly interactive moment of song, performed after the sharing of Eucharistic bread and wine, deepens their sense of "communion" one with another and with the One who is praised.

---

of Lourdes. However, the second community is beyond the scope of my research.

[8] Images taken from conversations with members of the Lourdes community.

Second, attention to music in this community's worship enables us to observe how processes of liturgical change and inculturation unfold, and therefore to reflect on how our liturgical traditions are being shaped and handed on.[9] What is striking in this community's worship is that neither liturgical texts nor structures have been a primary object of liturgical change. Rather, texts and structures have been elaborately embedded and contextualized in the community's song, word, and action. Music is especially significant: first, because music is pervasive within each liturgical event—including multiple songs, liturgical acclamations, and the piano improvisation that often undergirds prayers, ritual actions, and improvised speech—and second, because the affective power of gospel music performance shapes the style/ethos of the whole worship event, creating a spiritual and cultural resonance within which prayers, Scripture readings, and other liturgical texts are experienced. In addition, the process by which musical/liturgical change has taken place at Lourdes, and continues to evolve, is not determined by a single "authority" within the community, but is dependent on the intuitions of many members, notably musical leaders, who select music in light of the weekly Scripture readings, and, in the course of worship, shape the "feel," the timing, and the leadership of multiple musical moments. These intuitions have been honed over time through their own faithful practice, as they continue to learn "how to enter into the paschal mystery by embodying it ritually."[10]

Third, this community's musical practice expands the understandings of liturgical aesthetics and creativity currently operative in liturgical theology. Liturgical scholars associate music's role in worship with the aesthetic and creative dimensions of liturgical practice by which persons are opened to the "deeper mysteries of God and the human condition before God."[11] In so doing, they make two primary associations: first, aesthetic concerns are linked primarily to beauty; second, creativity is associated primarily with the action of the "artist."[12]

[9] Here I use some of Mary Collins' findings in her study of the evolution of profession rites among Benedictine women as a springboard for my own reflections. See Collins, "An Adventuresome Hypothesis."

[10] Ibid., 48.

[11] Saliers, *Worship as Theology*, 196. See also Irwin, *Context and Text*, 222.

[12] Irwin, *Context and Text*, 219–21.

Within the interpretive categories of the Our Lady of Lourdes community, as in the larger African American traditions of music and art, the experience of "soul" is a primary aesthetic and theological category. Here, "soul" is a point of critique and judgment about all that takes place in musical and liturgical performance. Beautiful singing is not adequate in itself. Without soul, a song's message is not delivered. Singers say that they must "dig deep" within themselves to touch the core of their own faith and their personal experience of the song's message, and then communicate it through an intense and soulful performance that weds vocal sound with bodily expressiveness. Without soul, music, word, or action lacks the power and dynamism necessary to communicate intimations of Godliness, holiness, and the Spirit's action that resonate with this community's spirituality.

Tracing the origins of this notion of soul, Clarence Rivers explains:

> The word "soul" used in the Genesis story of the creation of humankind . . . made sense to [our ancestors] in a very profound way, a story that fitted into their African religious view of the universe. Life, vitality, power, and dynamism were gifts of the Spirit of God; and in the Genesis story God breathed His Spirit into clay and thereby created a soul—an alive thing that reflected the power, vitality, and dynamism of God's Spirit. . . . Blacks have applied the term soul to any performance that is moving, or as they might say from a theological perspective, any performance that like the Spirit of God, inspires, moves, renews, breathes life into, . . . [is] power-filled.[13]

Likewise, current notions of liturgical creativity are expanded by the improvisatory art of the Lourdes' community, for whom the composed musical score is not the primary reference for performance. Rather, the creative action of God's Spirit is understood to move within the entire community, animating and shaping the improvisatory and highly interactive performance of any song or instrumental interlude. Musical creativity, in this context, is less the work of a single artist and more a communal event, even a mode of corporate spirituality.

[13] Clarence R. J. Rivers, *The Spirit in Worship* (Cincinnati: Stimuli, Inc., 1978) 29.

Fourth, in a striking way the ecclesial relationships that are mediated in this community's musical performance redefine the expected locus of liturgical authority, spiritual power, and wisdom in Roman Catholic liturgical events. Musical performers are recognized as liturgical leaders—carrying an authority to proclaim the Word musically and to give expression to the community's praise and thanksgiving. Many of those who take musical leadership are women. As musical performance unfolds, community members actively affirm the spiritual power and authority of these women musicians, especially those who serve as lead singers, through words of encouragement, through their engagement in singing/clapping/movement, and through their willingness to allow musicians to "shape" moments of the rite musically. At the same time, music making creates an inclusive continuum of action within which the Spirit's gifts in other members can be expressed, recognized, and confirmed.

A final challenge to current understandings of music as worship offered by this community's music making is linked to liturgical theologians' designation of worship as "sacred time" and "sacred space"; that is, time and space distinct from the realm of the secular. Conversations with members of the Lourdes community indicate that this sacred/secular dichotomy is not assumed. In their perception, all life and all time are sacred; God can and must be worshiped "at all times and in all places."[14] Thus, their action within the worship event reflects both the familial modes of care and love that are part of the rest of their lives and the expressions of praise and testimony which slip into their everyday speech: "Oh, have mercy!" "Thank you, Jesus!" In fact, they often speak of their liturgy as "having a good time in the Lord." Their use of gospel music further corroborates this lack of sacred/secular distinction. Gospel music performance, while powerfully religious in its message and intent, has never been restricted to liturgical contexts. Its religious vitality lies not in the distinction of its rhythms and stylistic elements from what might be considered secular music, but in its power to speak words of faith in the most concrete of human situatedness—pain, struggles, discouragement, as well as moments of intense joy.

---

[14] See also Joseph L. Howze, et al., *What We Have Seen and Heard: A Pastoral Letter on Evangelization From the Black Bishops of the United States* (Cincinnati: St. Anthony Messenger, 1984) 8.

I believe it would be more accurate to describe this community's liturgy as "church time" and "church space." This designation in no way undermines the centrality or profundity of God's action or self-disclosure in their worship. Nor does it deny that what takes place is sacred. Rather, it underscores that what is most characteristic of worship in this setting is that the action of God is inexorably bound up with the action of the community. It highlights that liturgy is fundamentally about being *"ekklesia,"*[15] the "convocation" of God which transforms the community's identity and empowers it to be the healing action of God one to another. What distinguishes this liturgical action/time/space from other action/time/space is that the "church" as convoked by God is gathered and acting. Through gospel music performance, the community integrates the world of worship and that of its everyday life, and enacts ecclesial relationships that flow from how God is understood to be present and active. "Being church" and "having church" are intimately related. One woman explains:

> What I mean by "having church" is that people have the freedom to be who they are. For us church is like a second home. We are the church. . . . People come to pray. . . . Some may sit in the back and be quiet, others may stand up and shout. If something is really heavy, if they need to pray out loud, the church prays with them. . . . The church is a community. We can pray, we can laugh, we can cry together, we can celebrate the joys, the strengths, and we do it all together. It's in song, in music, and within the liturgy.[16]

These insights about music *as worship* are a hint of the kinds of learning that might emerge from other studies of musical-liturgical performance. They demonstrate a process by which current understandings can be placed in fruitful dialogue with what is mediated in particular worshiping assemblies so as to deepen our understanding of how music is constitutive of liturgical action.

Reflections on Music as Theology

Theology, as we noted earlier, is about relationships, the deep spiritual relationships that mark a religious people—relationships

---

[15] Aimé Georges Martimort, ed., *The Church at Prayer*, vol. 1: *Principles of the Liturgy* (Collegeville: The Liturgical Press, 1987) 92–6.
[16] From an interview with a woman in the parish.

with God, with one another as ecclesial community, and with the rest of the human family. Insofar as musical performance evokes and enacts these relationships, engages persons in intuitions of God's presence and action within the church-at-worship, situates a community within its own political, social, and cultural history, and shapes their action in the world, it is an integral part of the theology embodied in worship.

Based on these assumptions, the second part of our dialogue might address these questions: What can be learned from a community's practice about music as theology? How does this community's musical performance confirm, expand, or challenge current understandings of the embodied theology mediated in worship? Here, the insights of contemporary liturgical theologians into six theological dimensions of Christian worship, understood to be perennial and enduring, can serve as a springboard for the exploration. Again, I will offer illustrations from my study of the Our Lady of Lourdes community,[17] and propose questions for exploring the practice of other communities.

Worship Music as Theological-Trinitarian

Liturgical theologians underscore that Christian worship is not only about God; more importantly, it is of God,[18] and therefore a profoundly theological act. It is a living encounter, a fresh experience of God's self-disclosure and self-communication, an emergent experience of God's action within the community. As noted earlier, each community's worship is a ritual encounter with the God of Christian faith—the triune God manifest in the person of Jesus Christ, now given over to the world and Church as Spirit. But how the action is experienced as the memory of Jesus, as the action of the Spirit, is uniquely mediated through the complex forms of human communication and action a community cultivates. Music, as one of the many "languages" of ritual action, can evoke a sense of "presence"—of God, of Christ, or the Spirit; it may communicate intimations of "Godliness" or "holiness." Frank Burch Brown corroborates

---

[17] For a fuller ethnographic presentation of the reflections that follow see McGann, "Interpreting the Ritual Role of Music," 71–241.

[18] See Kavanagh, *On Liturgical Theology*, 96–121.

this perception in his work on religious aesthetics, proposing that the styles of various performance media, including music, are a primary way by which a community "accesses a God who wills to approach and be approached," and thus are of profound theological significance.[19] He portrays the "performance traditions" of several Christian church bodies as indicators of how "'our' style and 'God's' style" of presence are related.[20]

Based on these perceptions we might ask, how are God's self-disclosure and self-communication described, understood, mediated, and experienced within a community's music and ritual performance? What new images of God's action emerge? Here it might be fruitful to explore the metaphors and images used by community members to describe their musical and liturgical performance. Do these qualities of performance relate in any way to how God is perceived to be present and active in the worship event? For example, members of the Our Lady of Lourdes community describe music as pulsing, moving, engaging, full of power and energy. Drums are essential to their performance as catalysts for movement. Singing and accompaniment styles are rhythmic, even percussive. In this context, music is meant to be "felt and not only heard," suggesting that members of the community perceive God's action in worship to encompass body and spirit, mind and heart—indeed the whole person. Thus, the qualities they identify and value in their musical idiom communicate something of how God is known—as "source of life, dynamism, and movement; of motion and emotion."[21]

Musical-liturgical style may also be significantly related to how Christian worship is experienced as Trinitarian.[22] It is striking that in contemporary Trinitarian theology, the early Christian image of *perichōrēsis*[23] has resurfaced as a crucial interpretive understand-

---

[19] Frank Burch Brown, *Religious Aesthetics: A Theological Study of Making and Meaning* (Princeton, N.J.: Princeton University Press, 1989) 125.

[20] Ibid., 117–35.

[21] Rivers, *The Spirit in Worship*, 22.

[22] See Corbon, *The Wellspring of Worship*, 1–74, on how Christian worship flows from the life of the Trinity.

[23] "*Perichōrēsis* means being-in-one-another, permeation without confusion. . . . To be a divine person is to be *by nature* in relation to other persons. Each divine person is irresistibly drawn to the other, taking his/her existence from the other, containing the other in him/herself, while at the same

ing.[24] Catherine LaCugna points out that the primary referent of this image is not how God is unto Godself, but how the triune God is "God-for-us." The attractiveness of this image to contemporary Christians resides both in the truth it carries of the mutuality of relationship among the three divine persons, and in the recognition that this mutuality is reflective of God's desire for human interrelatedness. Divine life is imaged as the dynamic flow of communication among persons, captured in the image of a "divine dance" at once "ecstatic, relational, dynamic, vital."[25] Implicit in this image of intradivine life and communication is a model for relationship among persons in the human community, one based on reciprocity, inclusiveness, mutuality, and freedom.

But how does this image of *perichōrēsis* as the dynamic flow of life and communication within God-as-Trinity-for-us relate to the images of God's action that are mediated in the music of particular worshiping assemblies? Does it find resonance in the styles of human interrelatedness created in musical and liturgical performance? Gospel music performance within the worship of Our Lady of Lourdes is highly interactive and dynamically communal in character. Musicians, situated in the sanctuary, face the rest of the assembly throughout the liturgy. On any given song, musical interaction among lead singers, instrumentalists, choir, and other participants is reciprocal and improvisatory, creating a dynamic and rhythmic flow of vocal, verbal, and gestural communication. Members of the community comment that within this flow of energy, the words of hope and encouragement articulated in a song enable them to be "re-centered in God," to move into a new experience of God's presence and faithfulness. Liturgical scholars might well access the "perichoretic knowing" of a community like this as resource for a

---

time pouring self out into the other. . . . There is no blurring of the individuality of each person, there is also no separation. There is only the communion of love in which each person comes to be what he/she is, entirely with reference to the other. . . . *Perichōrēsis* provides a dynamic model of persons in communion based on mutuality and interdependence." Catherine Mowry LaCugna, *God for Us: The Trinity and Christian Life* (San Francisco: Harper Collins, 1991) 271.

[24] See Elizabeth A. Johnson, *She Who Is: The Mystery of God in Feminist Theological Discourse* (New York: Crossroad, 1992) 220–1; LaCugna, *God for Us*, 270–8.

[25] LaCugna, *God for Us*, 271.

fuller understanding of the Trinitarian character of worship. But what of the music of other communities—what other metaphors for Trinitarian presence emerge? What relationships do these images bear to understandings of human interrelatedness, and how are these enacted musically as well as ritually?

Worship Music as Pneumatological

Contemporary liturgical theologians speak of worship as pneumatological and epicletic, although they admit that understandings of the active role of the Holy Spirit in worship have been considerably underplayed in Western liturgical theology for centuries.[26] In recovering images of the pneumatological character of worship, they make significant claims for how the Spirit is operative. They contend that liturgy derives from the action and power of the Holy Spirit,[27] that the church gathered for worship is radically dependent upon the Spirit of God to animate a liturgical assembly.[28] The Holy Spirit enables an assembly to take its constitutive role in the liturgical action[29] and orientates them toward God's future.[30] In the words of Don Saliers, "Without the life-giving, memory-conferring, and priestly-prophetic power of the Holy Spirit, no true thanks and praise will arise."[31]

But how does a worshiping community know, experience, and describe the Spirit's action? What role does music play in mediating that experience? What biblical images of the qualities of the Spirit's presence are evoked by their performance aesthetics? Here, the historical focus of the Black Church tradition on the pneumatological dimensions of worship, and the role of the Holy Spirit in music performance, have much to offer liturgical theology.

---

[26] See Irwin, *Context and Text*, 48; Edward J. Kilmartin, *Christian Liturgy: Theology and Practice*, vol. 1: *Systematic Theology of Liturgy* (Kansas City, Mo.: Sheed and Ward, 1988) 228–32; Mary Collins, "Eucharist and Christology Revisited: The Body of Christ," *Theological Digest* 39:4 (1992) 321–5; Corbon, *The Wellspring of Worship*, 65–74.

[27] Irwin, *Context and Text*, 48.

[28] Saliers, *Worship as Theology*, 67.

[29] Collins, "Eucharist and Christology Revisited," 324–5.

[30] Saliers, *Worship as Theology*, 136.

[31] Ibid., 117.

More specifically, in worship at Lourdes, there is a pervasive expectation that the Spirit will act within the liturgical gathering, which powerfully affects the performed structures and strategies of music making. For example, certain aspects of song performance are kept intentionally indeterminate—the number of repetitions of a refrain/verses, the particular vocal/verbal embellishments made by a lead singer, the length of a vamped repetition of phrases such as "Lord, help me to hold out!"—which allows the musicians to "build" and shape a piece in response to the movements of the Spirit within themselves and the assembly on a given occasion. Drum and piano accompaniments are likewise improvised. Singers speak of "God using them" to move and touch others through their singing. Preaching, praying, and singing are participative, with members of the community freely interjecting words/phrases such as "Yes!" "Amen!" "That's right!" as sung or spoken words affect them. All of this is understood as the necessary context for the Spirit's unpredictable action. In fact, members of the community describe music as key to how they experience the Spirit's animation. Music is said to "wake up the Spirit," to allow the Spirit to "heal burdens," and to "bring surrender to God." Images used by participants to depict the Spirit's action are similar to those they use to describe good musical performance: alive; causing fire, energy, heat, and movement; re-centering and changing persons; filling persons and the community; and bringing an experience of "one accord." In a remarkable way, these images reflect the biblical experience of the action of the Spirit, most particularly the pentecostal outpouring of the Spirit of God described in the Acts of the Apostles.

Worship Music as Sacramental: The Body of Christ

In speaking of Christian worship as *sacramental*, liturgical theologians frequently employ the image of the body of Christ. This theological image has multiple referents, two of which are directly linked to the presence of Christ in worship: the presence of Christ in his Spirit in the gathered assembly, and Christ's presence in the breaking and sharing of eucharistic bread and wine. Mary Collins raises a challenging question about the relationship of these two realities: How, she asks, can a community believe that the Lord Jesus will be sacramentally present in their eucharistic action if they have no religious experience of the Holy Spirit of the raised Christ among them?[32] She argues that the "beginning and end of the eucharistic action is the agapic love of the community of believers, the manifestation of the presence of Christ in Spirit."[33] This understanding is echoed by Louis-Marie Chauvet when he describes the eucharistic presence of Christ as a "crystallization" of Christ's presence in the assembly gathered in his name.[34]

If the action of the Spirit within a community is so central to belief in the sacramental presence of Jesus, do such realizations take place through music performance? How is the action of the Spirit in the lives of individuals and the community evidenced in the music making, and in the whole worship event? What experience of Christ's presence in the assembly is mediated in musical performance? Do new images of the body of Christ emerge? What role might music play in allowing Christ's presence to "come from the assembly," as Chauvet has proposed?

By way of illustration, musical performance is a primary way in which participants at Our Lady of Lourdes give personal witness to the action of the Spirit in their lives. Singers attest to the presence of Christ's Spirit within them by singing with power and conviction, through words of testimony interjected throughout a song or used to introduce it, and through vocal and gestural expressiveness which demonstrates that they are touched by a song's message. These modes of witness are contextualized by testimony given throughout the liturgy by those in leadership and other participants—who pray openly about their struggles and their reasons for gratitude; who address words of faith and encouragement to each other; and who acknowledge, through verbal acclamations and exuberant song, that the Spirit is acting.

Another acknowledged mode of the Spirit's presence is the experience of "communion" within the gathered assembly. During particular moments of music making, the Spirit is described by community members as having moved among them in a perceptible

[32] Collins, "Eucharist and Christology Revisited," 328. She grounds this question in what Peter Carnley identifies as the "structure of resurrection belief"—that Easter faith requires the "absolutely necessary empirical evidence" of the action of the Spirit of God in the community of believers. See Peter Carnley, *The Structure of Resurrection Belief* (Oxford: Clarendon Press, 1987).

[33] Collins, 330.

[34] Louis-Marie Chauvet, *Symbol and Sacrament: A Sacramental Reinterpretation of Christian Existence* (Collegeville: The Liturgical Press, 1995) 390.

way, effecting a sense of union that one participant images as the Spirit "incorporating the body." Often, this occurs during the extended period of song that follows the reception of the eucharistic bread and wine, as we noted earlier in the singing of "Perfect Praise." As with testimony, this experienced sense of communion, effected by the Spirit, becomes a lived context for the sacramental presence of Christ in the community's worship.

Worship Music as Biblical

In asserting that Christian corporate worship is biblical in character, liturgical theologians begin with the obvious: the proclamation and interpretation of biblical texts as integral to the worship event. But the biblical pattern of liturgy is not limited to proclamation and preaching.[35] Gordon Lathrop points out that the dynamic process by which liturgy juxtaposes the old and the new, so as to release new meaningfulness, is itself a profoundly biblical process. Old words and actions are made to speak with new grace.[36] Received ritual patterns are juxtaposed with the new image-breaking circumstances of a particular worshiping community. This process creates a set of generative associations, tensions, even conflicts within the worship event.[37] In this way, the "revelatory power of the tensions within the liturgical act" is released.[38]

Based on these perceptions we might ask: How does the community proclaim and interpret the biblical word through its musical performance? In what measure is the community's music making a carrier of new and image-breaking circumstances? How is it revelatory? What memory, associations, and tensions are released through music in the worship act?

Music and proclamation are integrally related in the worship of the Our Lady of Lourdes community. The lyrics of the songs performed are richly biblical in character. Images of the Lord as "my light and my salvation," "the Alpha and Omega," "my bright and morning star!" abound; passages such as Malachi 1:11 invite the community's praise:

[35] Gordon Lathrop, *Holy Things: A Liturgical Theology* (Minneapolis: Fortress Press, 1993) 15–32. See also Chauvet, *Symbol and Sacrament*, 190–227.

[36] Lathrop, *Holy Things*, 22–4.

[37] Saliers, *Worship as Theology*, 152.

[38] Ibid., 167.

"From the rising of the sun to the going down of the same, / The Lord is worthy to be praised!"[39] Old and New Testament imagery is often associated directly with the faith experience of those who sing:

> Oh, it is Jesus, Oh, it is Jesus,
> It is Jesus in my soul.
> For I have touched the hem of his garment
> and his love has made me whole.[40]

As in many African American communities, the interplay between song and preaching is explicit and multifaceted. Several singers speak of their musical art as a form of preaching. "We are not performers," comments one, "we are God's messengers. We are here to deliver a message." Singers strive to touch the biblical message within themselves, and to communicate their own personal experience of the message vocally and gesturally—through the quality/intensity of their sound and the movements of their bodies, allowing the word to take on personal and communal resonance. Thus, the biblical word is spoken/sung within the religious and social history of the community, providing a contextualization for the Word that is essential to God's self-revelation. The "place where revelation begins for Black people," notes theologian Shawn Copeland, "[is] in our own specific culture and ethos."[41] Within this community, musical performance is a primary bearer of the community's culture—its patterns of language and sound, its expressive modes of enactment, and its religious and social memory within which God is continually revealed.

At the same time, the cultural and religious memory evoked by musical performance is a memory shaped by oppression and exclusion both within and beyond the church context. Through musical performance, this community juxtaposes "new image-breaking" modes of expression that were formerly excluded from their Catholic Church practice—for example, the use of drums and the rhythmically generated gospel idiom—with the worship patterns of the larger Church. In so doing, they release what black theologian Diana Hayes

[39] Images taken from several songs.

[40] Text as sung, taken from "Oh, It Is Jesus," by Andrae Crouch.

[41] M. Shawn Copeland, "African American Catholics and Black Theology: An Interpretation," *Black Theology: A Documentary History*, vol. 2: *1980–1992*, ed. James H. Cone and Gayraud S. Wilmore (Maryknoll, N.Y.: Orbis Books, 1993) 110.

speaks of as "subversive memory." She reminds us that African American Catholics share the tradition of the Church from its earliest beginnings. Yet they critique that tradition, bringing a memory that

> can arguably be seen as "subversive," one which is paradoxical, turning all of accepted reality upside down to present a new reality, that of the last being called forth . . . as the bearers of a vital, healing vision . . . from their experience of both racial and religious persecution. They reflect the memory of a Church that has preached equality while practicing discrimination and segregation, a church that has preached a God of love while practicing racial hatred and division.[42]

Insofar as musical performance releases this subversive memory, it calls liturgical scholars to a "hermeneutic of suspicion"[43] regarding the historical evolution and the current practice of Christian worship. It calls attention to how the liturgical patterns fostered by the Church have excluded and silenced the gifts of some of its members; it questions whose voices have been missing from the Church's theologizing about its worship; and it invites a more inclusive mode of reflective theology that flows from the revelatory center which is the whole Church's worship.

Worship Music as Ecclesiological

Worship events, as understood by liturgical theologians, are actualizations of a community's identity as church, and are therefore ecclesiological.[44] In liturgy, the church becomes visible and audible—an epiphany of God's dwelling within the human community,[45] a "living icon of persons."[46] "The celebrating assembly," suggests Louis-Marie

---

[42] Diana L. Hayes, *And Still We Rise: An Introduction to Black Liberation Theology* (New York: Paulist Press, 1996) 173.

[43] Term taken from Elizabeth Schüssler Fiorenza, *Bread Not Stone: The Challenge of Feminist Biblical Interpretation* (Boston: Beacon Press, 1984) 15.

[44] See Kelleher, "Liturgy: An Ecclesial Act of Meaning," 482–97; Kelleher, "Liturgical Theology: A Task and a Method."

[45] Alexander Schmemann, *Liturgy and Tradition: Theological Reflections of Alexander Schmemann*, ed. Thomas Fisch (Crestwood, N.J.: St. Vladimir's Seminary Press, 1990) 55.

[46] Image taken from Robert Taft, "What Does Liturgy Do? Toward a Soteriology of Liturgical Celebration: Some Theses," *Worship* 66:3 (1992) 199.

Chauvet, "is the first place for the manifestation of . . . the church as the church of Jesus Christ, animated by the diverse charisms of the Spirit."[47] Perceptions of social and ecclesial relatedness become articulate within a worshiping assembly.[48] What emerges is a "a model of church," if you will.

What can liturgical theologians learn from the musical-liturgical performance of local communities about the models of church that are actually mediated in the living tradition? Within a particular community's liturgy, what ecclesial relationships are actualized through musical performance? What experience of the body as a whole, of the interrelatedness of its members, is evoked? How are these relationships understood and interpreted? What images of the Church, animated by the diverse charisms of the Spirit, come into play?

What emerges in the musical performance and in the whole worship event at Our Lady of Lourdes is a highly interdependent model of liturgy and of Church. The whole assembly is assumed to be essential to the Gospel style of music making, although the modes of musical participation are diverse—singing, rhythmic movement, clapping, gestures of testimony, spoken interjections, or quiet listening. The relationships that are actualized in musical performance, among musical leaders and within the whole performing assembly, are highly reciprocal and interactive in character—a continuous and complex form of "call and response." At times the musical-liturgical performance mediates a strongly unified body (Eucharistic Prayer acclamations); at others, diverse modes of participation allow great latitude for personal initiative and variation (extended exchange of peace). Modes of communal embodiment, of "being church," become most complex during particular moments of song, when various forms of personal expressiveness on the part of musicians and other members of the assembly are held in dynamic tension with strong, rhythmically unified musical action.

Worship Music as Eschatological

Finally, liturgical theologians claim that worship is an act of realized eschatology.[49] Worship situates a Christian community in rela-

---

[47] Chauvet, *Symbol and Sacrament*, 184.
[48] See Foley, "Toward a Sound Theology," 145–72.
[49] See Corbon, *The Wellspring of Worship*, 49–55.

tionship to the world, within the sphere of concrete human social-political history.[50] It expresses how this social body is related to the human project of being-in-the-world, and expresses its expectations of how the promises of God will be fulfilled within this history and beyond. In worship, a community opens to "a future beginning now, in this time and place,"[51] and to the role it might play in bringing God's promises for the world to fulfillment.

How is this claim evidenced in a community's musical and liturgical action? Do new images of God's action in history, of God's justice, emerge in musical performance? What do they teach us about how worship is eschatological? What expectations and longings for eschatological fulfillment are expressed? How does musical-ritual action empower persons to act in the larger social arena? Clearly, the particular social-political history and current context of each community will significantly affect the manner in which this eschatological dimension of worship is experienced.

In the practice of the Our Lady of Lourdes community, God's faithfulness in the midst of social and political struggle is often expressed and eloquently reiterated in moments of communal song:

> We've come this far by faith,
> leaning on the Lord,
> trusting in his holy word,
> He's never failed me yet![52]
>
> God of our weary years,
> God of our silent tears,
> Thou who hast brought us thus far on the way.[53]

These articulations of faith in the face of social structures which oppress both members of the community and numerous others within the larger social community are reiterated in preaching, prayer, and the testimony of participants. Characteristically, preaching both addresses those aspects of the community's lived experience which thwart life and acknowledges the power of God's Spirit to transform individuals and the community to act freely on their own

---

[50] Saliers, *Worship as Theology,* 49–68.

[51] Ibid., 68.

[52] Taken from "We've Come This Far by Faith," by Albert A. Goodson.

[53] Taken from "Lift Every Voice and Sing," by James Weldon Johnson.

behalf and the behalf of others; that is, to be defined by God's action rather than the structures of society. Within the whole schema of the event, the act of music making plays a unique role in this transformative process. Over and again, within the energy, joy, and communal interaction of musical performance, the sureness of God's action is reexperienced; the power of the Spirit is communally received, grounding a musically articulated vision that "[we] can't turn around!" but must "hold out" because "God is able," and "God will make a way where there is no way!"[54]

Musical performance is likewise a dynamic factor in the "redemptive reordering of relationships,"[55] both ecclesial and social, that occurs within the community's liturgical performance. Elder members of the community and children are invited to make specific contributions to the worship and music making. Women as well as men assume major roles of prayer leadership as lead singers, choir members, speakers, and through spontaneous testimony offered throughout the event. Young adults are encouraged to address the community about their hopes, fears, and struggles, and are constantly supported and encouraged. Lay and ordained members of the community take responsibility together for what takes place in worship and together rely on the action of the Spirit. The worship experience anticipates a new order of relationships, one which does not flow from the patterns of the wider society, but which is based in a valuing of the gifts and vision of each member. The fruit of this redemptive reordering of relationships within worship is the empowerment of participants for the work of reordering relationships within the larger social arena.[56]

[54] Images taken from several songs. James Cone contends that, within the Black church, worship has always provided the "connection between the experience of holiness . . . and the struggle for political justice in the larger society. . . . The divine Spirit, [who] is the power of Jesus . . . breaks into the lives of the people giving them a new song to sing as a confirmation of God's presence with them in historical struggle." See James H. Cone, "Sanctification, Liberation, and Black Worship," *Theology Today* 35:2 (1978) 139–40. See also Melva Wilson Costen, *African American Christian Worship* (Nashville: Abingdon Press, 1993) 119.

[55] See Mary Collins, "Principles of Feminist Liturgy," *Women at Worship: Interpretations of North American Diversity,* ed. Marjorie Procter-Smith and Janet Walton (Louisville: Westminister/John Knox Press, 1993) 13–14.

[56] Robert Michael Franklin, "Defiant Spirituality: Worship and Formation in the Black Churches," *Proceedings of the North American Academy of Liturgy* (1992) 15–21.

Within the whole sphere of this community's worship, lived and experienced as "realized eschatology," particular moments of communal song gather up the expectations of the community that, although the struggle to live in freedom is ever present, "Jesus' resurrection already defines what the ultimate outcome will be."[57] And in song, the community anticipates that eschatological fulfillment, expressed artistically and vividly through images such as being "ready when Jesus comes," because "I'm goin' up yonder to be with my Lord." In the words of one song, although burdens "press me down,"

> This old race will soon be over,
> and there will be no race for me to run, Lord.
> But as I stand before God's throne, all my heartaches will be gone
> when I hear my Savior say *"Welcome home!"*[58]

Whenever this song is sung, these lines release a moment of communal exuberance and joy in which the community anticipates eschatological fulfillment as "home" and "welcome."

Implications for the Future of Liturgical Studies

The method we have now explored in full carries several implications for the field of liturgical studies. First, it underscores the contention that music is integral and constitutive of liturgical action, and provides a practical method for testing this assumption within the actual worship of Christian communities. Moreover, it offers an approach to musical performance within worship events that focuses not only on musical texts, forms, and aesthetic qualities, but also on music as ritual action, on the performing assembly as subjects of the action, and on the interdependence of musical and liturgical processes. And it provides a strategy for exploring a theology of music that is consonant with our understandings of the theological dimensions of Christian liturgy.

Second, it opens the possibility that paying attention to culturally diverse music may be a key to discovering significantly new

---

[57] Cone, "Sanctification, Liberation, and Black Worship," 151.
[58] Taken from "Rough Side of the Mountain," by Rev. F. C. Barnes and Rev. James Brown Barnes.

dimensions of our lived traditions, and of perceiving how these traditions are being shaped and handed on to future generations. It invites liturgical scholars to explore musics that may reveal a subversive memory regarding the historical shaping of our rites and the musics by which they have been celebrated. And it provides a way of hearing and seeing the rhythms and sights of liturgical-inculturation-in-process, so as to understand better how we are being led into the future.

Third, the method we have just explored provides a way to bring our liturgical theory and theology into greater dialogue with practice. Given the appropriately normative posture of liturgical theology, and by implication, much of the work of liturgical studies, new models must continue to emerge for how empirical field research can be integrated into our frameworks of thought. This is especially true at a time when our churches' ritual life is marked by much greater cultural diversity than in our recent past. Liturgical scholarship risks losing relevance to the Church's lived experience of worship unless we more systematically invite the perspectives of communities and theologians who represent that diversity.

Fourth, this method images a more collaborative model for the work of liturgical studies, and a broader base for the work of reflective and critical theology. In so doing, it poses the question of who is "at the table" when liturgical theologizing takes place. And it offers one of many ways in which lay and professional "liturgical theologians" can be in dialogue. As Mary Collins has pointed out, local assemblies have gained their liturgical competence not through study or office but through faithful practice, by entering the paschal mystery "by embodying it ritually."[59] This method underscores the potential fruitfulness of the "border crossings" of which we spoke in the Introduction: the collaboration between liturgical scholars and local communities of faith. But, the challenge remains:

> Can experts like ourselves acknowledge that we do not know the future of our liturgical traditions and become companions to other believers who are working ritually to reconstruct faith and life? Will we be open to learning, when their judgements about what is authentic tradition do not seem to correspond with our expert opinions?[60]

---

[59] Collins, "An Adventuresome Hypothesis," 48.
[60] Ibid.

Finally, it raises questions about how we imagine the future work of our disciplines at this time of massive cultural change and global consciousness. How will future generations of liturgical scholars and theologians be trained for their role in the churches? What methodologies will enable them to undertake a theological task that is inclusive, collaborative, and global at its core? What cross-disciplinary strategies will equip them to draw insight from diverse communities, and from the multiple cultural and theological narratives they enact in worship?

At the time of Vatican II, and comparable events in other denominations, liturgical theologians and historians played a crucial role in reawakening the churches' liturgical memory and imagination.[61] Prior to the council, the restrictive practice of worship—both Roman Catholic and Protestant—had all but dried up our liturgical imagination. Academic liturgists played a role as strategists and shamans, inviting the Church into an initially unfamiliar liturgical future. Among the many fruits of their dedicated leadership is the process of liturgical inculturation that flourishes today in the churches.

Thirty-five years later, the very communities who have responded most fully to these initiatives hold a key to the exercise of liturgical memory and imagination. In many instances, music is central to how new intuitions of ecclesial identity are being mediated. Liturgical theologians need to be in dialogue with these communities so as to learn the creative dynamism they discover in their worship music. Liturgical historians need to attend to the historical memories awakened as musical and aesthetic styles once suppressed are rediscovered.

No doubt, the future lies in a plurality of liturgical theologies that reflect the diversity of the world church. Are we willing to undertake the experimental process by which these can emerge?

---

[61] Collins, *Worship: Renewal to Practice*, 75. Images that follow are drawn from this source.